Mama Nettie's Time to Love

Gail C. Fusco

Mama Nettie's Time to Love
by Gail C. Fusco

Printed in the United States of America

ISBN 9781609573799

www.xulonpress.com

11/05/2010

To: My Nephew

Anthony Augustine

I hope that this book will give
you inspiration as you continue to
minister to God's people. I hope too
that reading our family history and the
wonderful legacy left to us will give you
great joy. Love & Blessings
                                    Your aunt,

                                    Gail C. Kusco

Dedications:

To all the people who made this book possible:

Arnette T. Giles: I literally owe my life to this kind and loving woman. Without the encouragement, guidance and living example of my dear grandmother, I would never have become the strong, brave person that I am today.

Charles R. Giles: My grandfather was the constant father figure in my life who taught me to pray and expect miracles.

Arthur Phillip Clementin III: My brother Art and I have always had the same heart and the same sentiments. I thank him for his input and collaboration on this venture, but most of all, I am just happy that he is my brother.

Neal V. Cook: Art introduced Neal to me as his adopted brother back in 1989. I truly would have never written this book without his constant encouragement and push. Thank you, my brother.

Mary and Sollie Mitchell: You have been my guardian angels and my best friends. Thank you for your countless acts of kindness and love over the past seven years. You have truly filled the void that I've felt in my life since the loss of my grandparents.

To My Children: Craig, Julie, Shaun, Jeremy and Mark, you are all my inspiration and the reason that I get up every morning. I love you all.

To My Ancient Relatives of the Choctaw Nation: Thank you for the spirit to endure.

Table of Contents

Introduction

Hurricane Katrina

On August 29, 2005, the layout of most of the lovely Mississippi Gulf Coast was washed away by a 30-foot storm surge when Hurricane Katrina devastated the shores of my homeland.

My younger brother, Art and I spent our early childhood in Pearlington, Mississippi in the home of our maternal grandparents. The town is located just 26 miles east of New Orleans, and it is situated on the Pearl River that serves as the southern and westernmost border between Mississippi and Louisiana.

When I was eight years old, Art and I left Pearlington and moved with our mother to Bay St. Louis, Mississippi. The Bay, as the locals call the town, is exactly 18 miles east of Pearlington, and for the first 35 years of my life, I never ventured more than 40 miles in either direction from that area.

As far back as I can recollect, Pearlington was a sleepy little hamlet where I passed the best years of my youth with my grandparents. During my childhood, Pearlington seemed like a giant place to me. However, by the time I was ten, I would come to realize that my sheltered little kingdom was nothing more than a one-horse town.

I must admit, back then, I had absolutely no clue about the former importance of the place. Much later I would learn that Pearlington had actually served as a catalyst to the productivity and industrialization of a wild territory that would eventually become a significant part of the great state of Mississippi. Pearlington would hold this position of importance for over 100 years. My little town, with her strategic location on the waterway, had carved a pathway into Mississippi's very history.

As young adults, our lives took different paths. Art and I both managed to get as far away from Pearlington as we could. I wound up in Rome, Italy, and Art spent 35 years of his life in Michigan. However, there will always be something compelling that attracts us back to Pearlington. Whether it's the call of ancient spirits or the land where we laughed and cried, Pearlington will always be our home, our roots.

When I moved back to the States from Europe, I spent a couple of years in Art's new hometown of Jackson, Michigan. We needed some time together to make up for all the years of separation.

Our grandparents were gone now, and our mother, Shirley was the only family we had left in Pearlington. So, we still had one tie to the land, and a reason to go home. By 2003, Mama had passed. The only two things that bound us to Pearlington were the side-by-side tomb of my grandparents which Mama's older brother, Eugene, and Art had built, and the rolling, muddy waters of the Pearl, where Mama's ashes were tossed.

After 35 years of Michigan snow, my brother had retired and returned to the Mississippi Gulf Coast. He took up residency in Bay St. Louis, and oddly enough, I made a trip from my home near Orlando, Florida to visit him just two days before Hurricane Katrina hit.

My oldest son, Craig, set out that Friday night on August 26th, driving from his home in Racine, Wisconsin to join me at my brother's house. We had planned a reunion months before, and Craig had taken his vacation in hopes of wetting his line off the fishing pier at the end of Ulman Avenue in Bay St. Louis.

Art and I stayed up all night Saturday, August 27th watching the weather channel as they tracked the storm.

Katrina swept across the southern tip of Florida and worked her way out into the Gulf of Mexico. Even though she was classified as a Category One storm over Florida, she had caused considerable havoc there. Now, in the boiling hot waters of the Gulf, storm prognosticators were predicting intensification and eminent doom for the Louisiana and Mississippi shores.

Art gave out about 1:00 a.m., and went to his room for a nap. I was more worried about my son on the highway than I was about the storm. I stayed fixed in front of the television and moved uncomfortably from the couch to the floor in an attempt to find some relief for my aching back. I knew that there would be no fishing excursions for anyone this trip. I laughed to myself as I thought how much smarter fish are than people, because they would definitely be headed in the opposite direction with a storm brewing as intensely as this one.

Craig arrived about 3:00 a.m. I unlocked the glass storm door and he stepped in, gave me a tight squeeze and planted a kiss on my cheek. He had listened to the weather on his radio, and I could tell by the grim look on his face that something was wrong.

"Mom, we've got to get the blazes out of here, that storm is headed straight for us."

"Well," I said, "I don't think your uncle is planning to leave. Besides, you've been driving for 20 hours. You need some rest, and I'm exhausted, too. Let's talk about this later, I need some sleep." I retired to the spare bedroom, and was just about to fall into a deep sleep when Craig called me again.

"Mom, get up. That storm is getting worse. We really need to get on the road. I'm taking you back to Florida."

I grumbled to myself. "I need some sleep, and just why is it that my kids think that they're my parents? They're always telling me what to do or what I need to do or when to do it. When did these roles get reversed, anyway?"

Like an obedient child, I walked into the living room. Art and Craig were having a discussion about putting up the storm shutters. "Unc, I'll help you get your shutters up and then we better all leave here."

About an hour later, Art's friend, Gene Jackson called from Tennessee. "Boy, you better get on that road and head this way, and I'm not taking no for an answer." Gene had taken Art under his wing when he moved from Mississippi to Michigan. He was more like a father, rather than a good friend, and Art knew that telling him no was absolutely out of the question.

I left Bay St. Louis with Craig around 9:30 a.m., Sunday morning, but by that time, it was already too late. The roads were jammed with evacuees. The usual nine-hour trip turned into 15 hours. There were periods of sitting at a standstill for hours on Interstate-10 between Bay St. Louis and Pensacola, Florida.

My two daughters, Julie and Shaun, were both in Louisiana. Julie lived on the west bank of New Orleans, and even though she was far enough from Lake Pontchartrain, her home was just a short distance from the Mississippi River.

Shaun left Lacombe, Louisiana on Saturday morning and drove west towards Baton Rouge. She encountered worse traffic problems than we had with our eastern escape the following morning, but she made it safely to Baton Rouge and found lodging at a hotel. Julie joined her there the following day.

Julie's husband, Bernard was a New Orleans police detective, so he was forced to stay behind and eventually wound up locked in the Super Dome, where he remained on duty for seven straight days.

My mother's oldest brother, Eugene Giles, lived in the seventh ward of New Orleans East for 45 years. His home was situated only a few blocks from Lake Pontchartrain and about a mile from the Industrial Canal. He and his family went to Lake Charles, Louisiana to escape the storm, so I knew they were safe.

I had more relatives in New Orleans from my father's side of the family: my cousins, Joan and Ronnie, and their families. Joan's son attempted to take her with him to Texas, but she refused to leave because she couldn't take her dog with her. So, he put her up in a hotel on St. Charles Avenue and left. Ronnie was disabled, but he lived with one of his daughters, so I felt comfortable thinking that she would care for him. The only family member we could not contact was our acquired uncle, LeNard Peters. Nearly two months would pass before we learned that his companion had taken him to Tennessee before the storm struck.

I stayed glued to the television, computer and telephone for the following six weeks. Shaun was able to call me daily because my cell phone was on her family plan, and for some strange reason, our phones worked. Eventually, Art drove from Tennessee to Alabama, where he and my sister-in-law stayed with her daughter in Mobile.

Once the roads were opened, Art made his way back to Bay St. Louis to check on his house. Most of the homes and businesses from the railroad track to Highway 90 received floodwater damage from the storm surge that came from two directions (the gulf waters of the beach, and the Jordan River). My brother's house was filled with water as the two rushing currents slammed into each other right in front of his door. It was as if Moses had just closed the Red Sea.

This fact was recounted by his sister-in-law, who rode out the storm in the cul-de-sac directly behind his.

Unfortunately, the roads were too debris-filled for him to make any assessment of the rest of the area. From what little I could see on television of the Gulfport-Biloxi area, there was probably not much left of the rest of the coastal towns. Clermont Harbor, Lakeshore, Ansley and Pearlington were never or barely mentioned by the media.

I was especially concerned about Pearlington. We never heard a word about that place on the news, and no one could get through the cluttered roads to report on the condition.

I saw footage of cemeteries in nearby Slidell, Louisiana where coffins had washed out of their graves and were now standing, propped against pine trees.

I began having nightmares about the tomb of my grandparents. The coastal region is some 13 feet below sea level, so whenever you dig a hole in the ground, you don't have to go very deep before hitting a pool of water. I knew how my grandmother feared water, and I could hear her voice in my dreams as she said, "Don't let them bury me underground, I would never want to be in that muddy water."

Yes, I was surely worried about my dead folks, but more so, my thoughts and concerns were for the living people whom I knew and loved there. I wanted to get to Pearlington.

Some six weeks after Katrina's passing, enough debris had been cleared to open the main roads. I made many anxious phone calls to my brother in Mobile until he did get to Pearlington and the surrounding area.

I was elated to learn that our grandparents' gravesite was unharmed. Their church, Holmes Chapel United Methodist, sustained some roof damage and structural damage to the new addition. The church was filled with floodwaters, but the mud could be washed out. The church was still standing.

My old parish, St. Joseph's Catholic Church was completely destroyed. The church was washed off its foundation and had to be demolished to remove it from the middle of Highway 604.

Our original homestead on Hancock Street, "the old house" remained intact, but the floodwaters rushed through and made it list to one side like an old sinking ship. My grandparents' second house, that faced Whites Road and sat on a lot directly behind the old house, was washed off its foundation and lay crumbling.

Most of the homes between Highway 604 and the Pearl River were destroyed. Nearly the entire town was submerged under the 25 to 30-foot surge of water that flattened everything in its path.

The town of Waveland was no more. Coleman Avenue (the town's main street, which ran nearly a mile from Beach Boulevard to the railroad tracks) was flattened. Nearly every home and business from the beach to the railroad tracks was gone or ruined by floodwaters.

Gulfside Assembly, which belongs to the United Methodist Church, was completely destroyed. Ironically, they had just dedicated the construction of new condominiums on the site exactly one week before the storm struck.

Bay St. Louis, Mississippi is the town where I spent the second half of my childhood. We lived just two blocks from the beach at 240 Washington Street. It was there that I shared an odd-looking pink house with my mother, stepfather, and baby sister, Faith.

Beach Boulevard (I referred to as Beach Road) was completely destroyed. All of the beautiful, old homes and businesses along the beach no longer existed.

The Bay Bridge that connected Bay St. Louis (Hancock County) to Pass Christian (Harrison County) along Highway 90 was completely destroyed. Every section of concrete was washed away.

The Hancock County Court House was damaged. The Hancock County Historical Society, where I did most of the research for this book, was miraculously spared. "Not a single record was lost," said Charles Gray, the Executive Director.

Although I trusted my brother's account of everything that had happened, nothing could have prepared me for the actual sight of the aftermath of Hurricane Katrina. I finally did go back nearly two months later. Sure, I was happy to learn that my family, friends, and nearly all the good people of the area had survived. I told myself that material things didn't really matter, until I actually saw what was left.

The devastation was too horrible. It took my breath away, and I was speechless. Not even a moan came from my throat. I could only gaze in awe as tears flowed down my cheeks. It was gone. There wasn't a limb or stone left that I had known. Everything was twisted. Everything was different. Everything was unfamiliar. The tall pines and fat oak trees stood shortened and naked. Plastic bags and clothing now hung from what was left of their trunks and limbs. There was no greenery, no grass, and no life. Not even a bird flew by.

After driving around Bay St. Louis, and what was left of Waveland, I headed out to Pearlington with Art. We drove in from Whites Road and stopped to survey my dear friend, Betty Arnold's place. Her lovely brick home was snapped in two like a matchstick and pushed off its foundation.

Betty told me a harrowing story of how her son, Darrel, along with his fiancé, had rescued her from the house when the floodwaters began to rise. She said that within seconds, the water rose to the window level. Darrel and his fiancé jumped from the window to get to his boat that was tied up in the back yard. By the time they made it back to the house, the water was at the roofline. He managed to reach through the window and pull his mother to safety. Betty, Darrel and his fiancé remained in the boat while the floodwaters rose to 30 feet. Later, they showed me the notch in the top of a pine tree where Darrel had tied the boat until the floodwaters began to recede.

We stopped on Whites Road to talk to other survivors who were sitting outside their tents along the side of the road. We passed Mama's old house, which had washed completely across the driveway and sat twisted on the fence that had kept it from washing onto the empty lot next door. Just up the road a bit, we paused to see my grandparents' house. It too was washed off its foundation and just sat drooping to one side.

We continued our drive from Whites Road, turned left onto Highway 604, and drove straight out to Highway 90. Everything was gone. The new brick post office was flattened. Sheriff Ronnie Cuevas' brick home was flattened to the foundation. My dear friends, George and Margaret Ladner's brick home was gone for the most part, too.

"I've seen enough," I told Art. "Take me to the cemetery."

We got out of the van and made the short walk to the family plot. I quickly walked around the tomb of my grandparents to inspect every angle. It was airtight. Not a scratch. However, many of the graves around it were sinking, or the cement showed cracks.

It's a miracle, I thought. We walked around for a bit to check on the graves of other family members and we returned to the main family plot.

"You take all the time you want, Sis," Art said. "I'll be waiting in the van for you."

"Go ahead." I said. "I just want to spend a few minutes with the old folks."

I walked over to the waist-high tomb, leaned over the top and spread my arms out to embrace the two people on earth whom I had loved the most. Everything that was dear to me had bloomed from them and through their eyes.

As I stood there, leaning against the cold stone, I could still feel the warmth and glow of their eternal love, and my thoughts began to drift back to them and the influence that they would always have on my life and the lives of everyone who knew them.

Arnette Thelma Giles

1901-1976

Chapter I

My Maternal Grandparents

Mama Nettie

My maternal grandmother, Arnette Thelma Peters, was born on August 8, 1901 in Bond, Mississippi, up Highway 49, just northwest of Wiggins, Mississippi. She often told us that Bond was a famous place for two reasons: Dizzy Dean, the baseball star lived there; and it was her birthplace.

Everyone under the age of 40 called her Mama Nettie. She stood five feet, three inches tall, and had inherited the high cheekbones and defined jaw line from her half-Choctaw, half-French mother, Adelaide Maxson. Mama Nettie's father, Captain Phillip Peters, was Choctaw too. My grandmother always laughed when she told me that she had inherited her wide, flat feet from her father.

My grandmother had beautiful, black hair and dark eyes perched between slanted eyelids. Her lips were so perfect. They seemed to be shaped by a sculptor's chisel, and they were always curved in a pleasant smile. Her enchanting laughter always warmed my heart and made everyone else happy, too. Her skin was flawless, and her bosom was just the right contour to form comfortable cushions for our young heads.

She always wore an apron over her housedress, but when she got dressed up for church or to make a trip to the city, she would put on her prettiest dress, sweep her hair high on top of her head, and paint her fingernails crimson red to match her rouge and lipstick. She sure was beautiful, but to us, she was just our wonderful Mama Nettie.

No one could ever tell by her beautiful, smiling face that she had ever experienced an unpleasant day in her life. The truth was that Mama Nettie had endured a devastating childhood, but the memories of her father's love and her faith in God had given her the strength to endure, and overcome innumerable hardships.

Mama Nettie's parents, Mama Adelaide Maxson and Papa Phillip Peters, were married on November 16, 1899. Mama Adelaide had already given birth to a baby girl, named Eucharist, in August of 1898. My great-grandmother, Mama Adelaide, was a spoiled seventeen-year-old who was totally unprepared for motherhood, and definitely not ready to settle down as a housewife. Papa Phillip, who was six years older, adored her and was elated by the birth of his second child on August 8, 1901. They named her Arnette Thelma, and Papa Phillip called her his "Sweet Nettie." In 1904, Mama Adelaide gave birth to a son, and they named him Phillip, Jr.

Papa Phillip worked on the schooners as a young man, and when he became a boat captain, he ran schooners between Pearlington, Mississippi and New Orleans, Louisiana. Sometimes, he was absent for one to two-week periods whenever they made the long trips between New Orleans, Louisiana and Mobile, Alabama.

During one of Papa's trips to Mobile around 1907, Mama Adelaide left her three small children with a neighbor, and she abandoned her family. When Papa Phillip returned home, he docked his schooner at the Pearlington pier and slung his heavy canvas sack over his shoulder. He smiled to himself as he drew a puff of smoke from his scorched pipe, and began the four-mile walk up the dirt road towards home.

As usual, the sack was filled with gifts for his beautiful bride and his three children. He could hardly wait to kiss them all, and feel the tiny arms of his children around his neck and legs. It felt good to be home again, and he hastened his pace as he caught sight of the large oak tree in his front yard.

Papa Phillip walked through the house, but found no signs of life. It was only seven o'clock in the morning. Where could they be? He went into the kitchen and removed one of the heavy, iron discs from the cook stove. There were no hot embers, only cold ashes. No fire had been set for hours. His heart filled with panic. Had something happened to his family? Was one of the children sick?

Papa Phillip went out the front door and ran back down the road to his neighbor. He pounded on the door until Mrs. Cornelius cracked it open. "Have you seen my family?" Papa Phillip asked.

Mrs. Cornelius put a finger to her lips to silence him. She swung the door wide open and grabbed his hand to pull him across the threshold. "Shoo!" she whispered. "You'll wake your chillun." She took Papa into the kitchen and pointed to a chair. "Sit down, Phillip, while I fix you a cup of coffee."

"I don't want any coffee. Please tell me what's happened to my family."

"I'm going to tell you everything in a minute, young man, but first thing you need to do is sit down here and calm that old heart of yours right down. Everyone's just fine, and what you be needin' right now is some of my good coffee with a shot of Mr. Cornelius' strong home brew."

With that, Mrs. Cornelius turned to the stove and poured a cup of black coffee from a granite percolator. She reached to a shelf above her head and grabbed a mason jar filled with a clear white liquid and set them both on the table. Mrs. Cornelius sat across from Papa Phillip and poured a generous amount of the clear liquid into the coffee, and she slid the cup across the table to Papa.

"Now you take a couple of good swigs, and I'm going to tell you everything you be needin' to know."

Papa sat staring at Mrs. Cornelius with wide eyes as he followed her instructions and drank hearty gulps of the hot, spiked liquid. It burned all the way down to his stomach, and he knew that the sensation was coming from the one hundred proof, home-brewed corn liquor. He knew better than to try to argue with Mrs. Cornelius. She was a forty-eight-year-old black woman who stood eye-to-eye with him at six feet. Her mouth was filled with large, white teeth that reminded him of a horse every time she smiled or let out one of her bellowing laughs. Soon the warmth seemed to spread to the tense muscles in his neck and temples.

"Na, you look a might bit better," Mrs. Cornelius said. "Don't you go get yo sef riled up again, but what I'm about to say ain't gonna make you one bit happy. Three days ago, Adelaide comes over with all three of the younguns. She tells me that she can't be staying in this here place another day, and she asks me if I could be looking after your chillun 'til you gets home from the sea. Well, I told her that it weren't right for a mother to go off and leave her family likes she was as free as a bird.

"God never blessed Mr. Cornelius and me with our own chillun, but I show nuff know that a mother is spose to be loving her babies more than life itself. I tried to talk some sense into that gal, but I reckon she had her mind made up. I certainly twern't going to let her run off, and leave those poor angels in the house all alone. So's I told her, 'If you done made up your mind, I reckon thar ain't nothing that I can do about it. I'll take care of these babies until their papa gets home.' With that, she handed me a pillowcase with some of their clothes, and that's the last I seen of her. That was three days ago. Those poor babies have cried themselves to sleep every night. They want to know where their mama is."

Papa Phillip sat and listened in disbelief. He didn't know what to say. The words were frozen in his throat. ***This must be a bad dream,*** he thought. "Dear God, what have I done to deserve this misery?" he prayed.

Mrs. Cornelius reached across the table and pressed both of her large hands over his. They sat there in the quiet kitchen for a long while.

"I'm mighty beholding to you, Mrs. Cornelius. I guess I better take my children home now, and then I'm going to look for my wife."

"Listen Phillip, if there's anything that Mr. Cornelius and me can do to help, you just let us know. I'll go wake the chillun and get them ready to go."

Mrs. Cornelius placed her elbows on the edge of the table and pushed herself up from her chair. She headed towards the hallway, but stopped abruptly and turned her thick girth back toward Papa.

"By the way, I heard gossip from town that Adelaide took the schooner to Gulfport when she left here. You might want to start looking there."

Papa sat waiting in the kitchen. Within a few minutes, Mrs. Cornelius returned with the three children trailing behind her. When she stepped aside, they all went running and screaming into the arms of their father. Papa knelt in the middle of Mrs. Cornelius' kitchen with outstretched arms. He held them tightly while tears streamed down his face.

"Okay, let's go home now. You children thank Mrs. Cornelius for taking care of you."

"Thank you, Mrs. Cornelius," they cried in unison.

"Papa, where is Mama? She left us here, and she never came back," Eucharist said.

"Now you three stop fretting. I'm going to find Mama and bring her home. Everything is going to be just fine. We need to go home now. I've got surprises for all of you." Papa stood up and picked up Nettie and baby Phillip.

Mrs. Cornelius handed Papa the pillowcase with the children's things, and she gave him an approving nod and a hard squeeze to his forearm.

"Thank you again, Mrs. Cornelius," Papa said over his shoulder as he walked down the hallway to the front door.

Mrs. Cornelius stood in the doorway, and she watched with sadness as they walked to the gate and turned up the road to their house. She went back to the kitchen and took a big drink from the Mason jar. "Lord, help that family," she prayed.

The front door of the house was still standing wide open. Papa took the children inside, and they told him that their mama had been acting strange for a few days before she left them.

"She was always crying, Papa," Nettie said.

"She never wanted to get out of bed, and when we told her that we were hungry, she would scream and yell at us and start crying again. We didn't know what to do, Papa. I tried to fix something for us to eat," said Eucharist.

"You were a good girl to take care of your younger sister and brother," Papa told his older daughter. "Now, I want you to all stop worrying. Close your eyes, and no peeking until I tell you. Papa's got something for everyone."

Papa Phillip walked to the kitchen where he had left his canvas bag. He returned to the parlor and placed packages in front of each of the giggling children.

"Okay, open your eyes," he shouted. The children tugged at the thick, hemp-colored paper and twine until they had exposed their gifts.

"Oh, Papa, she's beautiful," Eucharist cried as she cradled a ceramic-faced doll in her arms.

"My baby is beautiful, too," Nettie said.

Phillip Jr. was too busy with his little wooden train to even make a sound. Papa forced a smile as he watched the joy in his children's eyes. This scene had always made him so happy in the past, but now, there was a dark shadow over this not-so-joyous homecoming.

Papa Phillip spent the next two days at home with his children. He cooked their favorite dish of hot grits with redeye gravy and thick chunks of roasted pork. His presence seemed to calm them down, but they continued to inquire about the whereabouts of their mother. For the first time in their short lives, Papa could not give them an honest answer.

On the third day, Papa went down the road with the children to see his cousin, Moses Peters. Moses and his wife, Mamie, lived in the central area of Pearlington near the cemetery. Mamie took the children into the kitchen to give them a snack, while the two cousins sat in a wooden swing on the back porch and smoked their pipes.

"You've probably already heard the gossip around town. Adelaide's run off and left me and the children," Papa said to his cousin.

"Yep! The old hens have been cackling up and down the road. It's pretty hot news in town these days," Moses replied. "Didn't you see this coming?" He asked Papa.

"No, I didn't. You know that Adelaide's always been spoiled and headstrong. I guess it's my fault, too. Maybe I should have been firmer with her, stood up to her more. I just love her so much. I thought that I could make her happy by giving her everything that she wanted," Papa said.

"I told you a thousand times, Phillip. A man needs to let a woman know who's the boss from the start. That Adelaide has been wearing the pants so long that you've forgotten how to be a man."

Papa sat and listened to his older cousin's criticism.

"That's all well and good, and there's no need in crying over spilled milk. What I need to do right now is to go find my wife and try to talk some sense into her. I plan to bring her back. I need her, and my children need their mother. Would you and Mamie mind keeping my children until I get back?"

"Now you already know that won't be a problem," Moses replied. "Mamie loves those children as if they were her own. Mark my words, Phillip, if you don't knock some sense into that crazy woman's head, bringing her back to Pearlington is not going to make a dab bit of difference."

Papa Phillip returned to his cousin's house the following morning to drop off his children, and he caught the seven o'clock schooner to Gulfport. He already knew all of the sailors and workers along the dock in Gulfport, so it was easy to follow Mama Adelaide's trail. By early afternoon, he had traced her to a boarding house, which sat less than a mile from the port.

Papa entered the boarding house and approached a long, mahogany counter. No one was in sight, so he tapped the silver bell that sat on the counter.

"Coming, coming," a woman's voice shouted from the next room. A few seconds later, a tall, thin woman stepped behind the counter and peered at him over thin spectacles. "What can I do for you sir?" she asked in an irritated tone.

"I'm looking for someone," Papa replied, "and I was told that she's here."

"This is a respectable place," the woman replied indignantly. "No men are allowed in the rooms."

"The woman is my wife, Madam," Papa said. "I returned home a few days ago, after being out to sea for nearly two weeks. When I got home, I learned that my wife had left our three children with neighbors and run off. I've come to take her home."

"Well, I never!" the woman replied. "Now we don't want any trouble here. I reckon it's okay if you go up to talk to her, but if I hear one peep of trouble, I'm going to fetch the sheriff. Do you hear me?"

"There won't be any trouble. I assure you," Papa said.

"Up the stairs, last door on the left," replied the woman. "You be quiet about it!"

Papa Phillip bowed his head to the lady and turned to walk up the long stairway. He stayed in the center of the long, worn runner. The old rug reminded him of the thick carpet of straw, leaves and twigs that covered the floor of the forest. When he was a boy, his Choctaw father had taught him how to walk quietly through the thick carpet of the forest. He learned to remain undetected when they went into the woods to hunt for deer and wild boar. He tried to remember those steps now as he attempted to avoid the creaky boards of the hallway.

Finally, he reached the door. He stood there for a few minutes and took deep breaths of the stale boardinghouse air. Papa made a gentle rap on the door, and without waiting for an answer, he turned the crystal doorknob, and stepped into the room. Mama Adelaide sat on a stool in front of a vanity mirror. Her waist-length chestnut hair cascaded over her shoulders and covered the top portion of her white robe. Her porcelain skin looked translucent in the afternoon light. Papa entered the room and gently closed the door behind him.

Mama Adelaide looked at him in the mirror and began brushing her hair. "So, you found me," she said.

"It wasn't that difficult. There aren't that many beautiful women in these parts. Can you please tell me why you did this? Why did you leave our children, and our home?"

"I don't want to talk about it," Mama Adelaide replied. "I just want you to go away, and leave me alone."

"What are you talking about, what is wrong with you? You're coming home. Whatever this is, we can work it out, but your place is with our children and me. Now get your things. Let's go." With that, Papa grabbed Mama Adelaide by the wrist as she continued to squeeze the handle of the hairbrush. He pulled her around to face him, and knelt at her feet as he gripped her thighs. "Please stop this madness. Let's go home."

"Home, what do you know about home? You're never there. You leave me for days and weeks at a time. I'm stuck in that house with your brats, slaving from sunrise to sunset. I have no time to see my friends. I have no time to dance, no time to laugh and no time to have fun. I'm sick, sick, sick of it, I tell you. I've had enough, and I'm not going back."

Papa stared back at her in disbelief. "I make good money by working on the schooners. I need to work to take care of you and the children. I love you. Your children love you. Doesn't that mean anything?"

"No, it doesn't. I don't want you, and I don't want your children. They're yours, not mine. The buzzards laid them, and the sun hatched them. Now, get out. Leave me alone. I never want to see any of you again."

A chill ran through Papa Phillip. Mama Adelaide's words had stabbed him through the heart. He felt drained. His broad shoulders dropped into a slump, and the smile that had always curled his lips seemed to fade from his memory.

Without another word, he rose to his feet, and walked out of the room, down the stairs and out to the street. He walked for hours as he tried to make some sense of the last four days. He was hurt to learn that she no longer loved him, but the most painful words were the awful things that she had said about his children. Eventually, he returned to the port in time to catch the evening boat back to Pearlington.

As I thought about what Papa must have felt, my mind slipped back to a period in my own life when I, too, had actually heard Mama Adelaide repeat those painful words to her daughter.

I was sixteen years old when I personally witnessed one of Mama Adelaide's despicable rampages. That sunlit afternoon, Mama Nettie was standing on her back porch, and Mama Adelaide was standing at the back gate. As I approached them, I could hear that Mama Adelaide was screaming at her daughter, and in a burst of sheer meanness, she said it. "I've always told you, you're not mine, because the buzzards laid you and the sun hatched you."

I was enraged, and as I reached the gate, I could see the big tears rolling down Mama Nettie's face.

"Shut your mouth, you evil witch," I screamed. "I won't let you hurt my grandmother another day. Shut your mouth now or I promise, I'll kill you where you stand."

Mama Adelaide turned to me and said, "Come on, you young whippersnapper. I'm just as good now as the day I turned sixteen. I'll beat you to a frazzle."

I bent down and picked up an old glass Coca Cola bottle, and I made a step towards the madwoman.

Just then, Mama Nettie yelled to me. "No, don't. It's all right. Now put down that bottle and come on inside."

As usual, Mama Nettie's voice had a calming effect on me, and I joined her on the porch, and put my arm around her waist. For years, my grandmother had told me about the painful memories of her mother's verbal abuse, and finally I witnessed it for myself.

That day after he heard Mama Adelaide say that, Papa didn't know what to do, but he knew that he had to take care of his children. He was running schooners for Captain Joseph Favre, and he asked if he could be relieved from the long schooner runs. He was allowed to continue the short mail trips between New Orleans and Gulfport. Meanwhile, he tried to spend as much time with the children as possible. He left them with his cousin's wife, Mamie, or his neighbor, Mrs. Cornelius, when he went off to work. Eventually, Papa was placed back on the schedule for the long trips to Mobile, and he was faced with making a decision to find a more permanent solution for the children.

Cousin Moses and his wife, Mamie, took in nine-year-old Eucharist; Mama Nettie's younger brother, Phillip Jr., went to live with a Pearlington resident named Oris Nelson and his wife, Mary; and Papa hired a housekeeper who moved in with him and took care of Nettie.

In the first eight years of her childhood, Nettie would learn enough about love and kindness from her father to help her survive many years of agonizing heartache. The children remained separated, and when Papa Phillip was forced to leave his young daughter for longer periods, Nettie was shuffled about between various relatives.

My grandmother suffered a lot as a child, but her worst memories were while living in Mobile, Alabama with Papa Phillip's older sister, her abusive Aunt Hettie. Under her aunt's supervision, Mama Nettie lived a true Cinderella story. She was forced to sleep on a bed of straw in the kitchen, while her two cousins, Emma and Frances, slept on fresh, white linen every night. Of course, my grandmother was forced to wash and iron those linens, and care for the household. She was allowed to leave the house only to act as a chaperone for her equally unpleasant cousins.

Around 1917, the three girls were out strolling near Mobile Bay, and they met a young foreigner named Carmelo. He was a sailor off one of the ships from South America. They struck up a conversation with Carmelo, and eventually the girls gave him their address. From then on, whenever Carmelo's ship made port at Mobile Bay, he rushed to the house to pay a visit.

During one of his visits, Aunt Hettie asked, "Carmelo, you've been coming to my house for a long time. Now tell me, which one of the girls are you coming to see?"

Carmelo replied in his broken English accent, "Oh, I come to see me darling, the pretty one!"

"But which one is she? Which one is your darling?" asked Hettie.

"That one!" replied Carmelo, and he pointed his index finger towards my grandmother.

A hush fell over the room, and loud shrieks were emitted from the two envious cousins. Mama Nettie sat frozen in her chair, and fear spread across her chest because she knew that there would be retaliation from her cruel relatives.

"Nettie, did you know about this?" asked the mean aunt.

"Why no ma'am, I did nothing to encourage him."

"She's right. I didn't even tell her how I feel, but since you insisted, now you all know who it is that I love," Carmelo said.

It was the custom for young girls to be chaperoned at all times whenever they were in the company of young men. However, they were allowed to walk a few steps ahead of the adults. This gave the couple brief moments to whisper secrets and promises. Nothing of this sort had ever happened between this phantom couple.

From that day on, Aunt Hettie accompanied the three girls whenever they were allowed to go out, and she made certain that Mama Nettie and Carmelo were never allowed any contact.

If it's true that absence makes the heart grow fonder, it certainly worked for Carmelo, but after a while he disappeared, and Mama Nettie thought Aunt Hettie had finally managed to run him off.

Nearly a year later, there was a knock at the door. A middle-aged Hispanic lady introduced herself to Nettie, and said that she was Carmelo's mother. She had traveled all the way from South America to tell my grandmother that her son had been killed in an accident at sea. They stood there in the doorway for a long period before Aunt Hettie appeared.

"Who is it?" Hettie asked.

"I'm Carmelo's mother," the woman replied.

"Well, come in please, and make yourself comfortable," Aunt Hettie said with a big, hospitable grin spread across her face.

"I don't mean to disturb you, but I'm in mourning for my son, Carmelo, who was killed at sea nearly a year ago. He told me about his love for Nettie and his desire to marry her. I wanted to meet her in person, and I just want to know if she ever received the hope chest that Carmelo and I sent to her?"

"You sent me a hope chest?" Nettie asked.

"Why yes! We sent a beautiful wooden trunk filled with linens and gowns for your wedding."

"I never received anything," my grandmother replied.

"Well, they were received and signed for by someone in this house." She turned to Aunt Hettie with a knowing glare. "Do you know about this?" she asked.

Finally, the despicable aunt admitted the truth. She had indeed received the hope chest and divided its contents between her two daughters.

"May I have a moment alone with Nettie?" asked Carmelo's mother.

"Well, I guess it will be all right," snapped the wicked one, and she turned and walked from the parlor in a huff.

The two women sat and held hands for a long time, and they both cried for the son, and the friend, lost at sea. After a while, the mother kissed Mama Nettie and departed.

Mama Nettie sat for a long while thinking about Carmelo. She did not have the same affection for him. They had never even been allowed to hold a private conversation. However, under different circumstances, perhaps he would have been the love of her life. Now, she would never know.

Mama Nettie vowed that day to remove herself from that pernicious house. Within a few months, in 1918, she met and married a man named Peter Daniels. She was only seventeen years old. They had a daughter the following year, and the marriage drew to an end before it got started. Mama Nettie took her baby, Myrtle, and left Mobile after the divorce. She went back home to Pearlington, and stayed with Papa Phillip in the house where she had been so happy as a little girl before her mother had abandoned them.

The Prophesies

Mama Nettie always had strange dreams, and shortly before leaving Mobile, she had a very weird experience. In a dream, she saw herself walking down a sidewalk. She looked ahead, and saw two young women coming toward her. One was dressed in a navy blue dress with white polka dots, and she wore a large white hat. The two women held their heads together, and they began to laugh when they looked at her. Just as the women were about to pass her, they stopped and turned in her direction. They both let out a burst of laughter, and one of them said, "Mr. Giles don't want you, because your feet are too big." They began to sing the same words in unison as they walked away.

Less than a year later, she did in fact meet Mr. Giles in Louisiana. One day, she stepped out of the Five and Dime Store in Slidell, and when she looked up, who did she see? It was none other than the two laughing women from her dream the year before. Just as she saw it in the dream, they began to laugh at her, and they sang that mean little song, "Mr. Giles don't want you because your feet are too big."

That dream would not be the last of its kind. Mama Nettie would be gifted with dreams and premonitions throughout her lifetime. I don't recall a single one that did not come to pass.

One of the most profound instances occurred when she stopped her youngest son, Charles, from going out one Saturday night. He really wanted to go, but when he saw the tears welled up in his mother's eyes, he hugged her around the neck and gave her a big kiss.

"Okay, Mama! I'm feeling pretty tired anyway. A good night's sleep will do me good. Wake me up so I can go to church with you and Dad tomorrow morning."

As soon as they got to the church that Sunday morning, they were greeted by a group of elders standing outside under the little bell tower.

"Well, thank God that you were not out with your buddies last night, Charles!" said Mr. Eddie Hurger. "We heard that there was a shooting at that juke joint where you boys hang out on Saturday nights. A couple of them young friends of yours are laid out on a slab as cold as a dead man's heels this morning."

Uncle Charles grabbed his mother's hand and gave it a hard squeeze. "Thank you, Mama," he whispered.

"*Thank you, Jesus* is what we need to be saying," Mama Nettie replied.

Uncle Charles placed his right hand on his chest, and raised his elbow. His mother slipped her hand through the loop in his arm, and they walked into the church.

I know very little about Uncle Charles. He was sickly as a child with asthma, and I vaguely remember him as a young man when I was a child. He had long, straight black hair that he wore combed back, and tied in a ponytail. I remember his visits from New Orleans. He would come to see his parents, and sometimes he would take a nap on the same chaise lounge that my father used when he came to visit us. I remember, too, that Mama Nettie prayed often for his health to improve.

Uncle Charles was very handsome, and when he went out in New Orleans, he wore nice double-breasted suits, wing-tipped shoes, and his head was always crowned with a fedora. His appearance made the women swoon, and he enjoyed accommodating them.

Uncle Charles, whom I called "Ankie," settled down and got married in June 1953, and had three beautiful children with his wife, Marion Davis. Unfortunately, they divorced in later years, but he stayed near, and took good care of his two stepchildren: Dorinda and Wilfred (Butch) Randall; and his three children: Charles, Jr. (Chuck), Michelle, and Adrienne.

He ran a janitorial service, and cleaned office buildings at night. Uncle Charles spent most weekends with his baby sister, Shirley, and they fished, and shared their love for vodka. If Mama drank a quart a day, Uncle Charles drank a gallon. In fact, we lovingly called him "El Taaka," which was his favorite brand of the Russian drink. He suffered a massive heart attack and died on September 4, 1985.

On Labor Day, around 1965, Mama Nettie told my brother, Art, "Son, don't go out tonight. I have a bad feeling that something is going to happen."

My brother stayed home that evening, and the next morning they learned that his friends were involved in a fatal auto accident.

Mama Nettie's dreams were not always woeful. She did have many premonitions of happy events, too.

There was one reoccurring dream that struck joy or fear into every female member of the family. My grandmother would dream that she was standing on the bank of a river, fishing. She would begin to pull in a big fish, and then she would see a woman walking along the opposite shore. If Mama Nettie called to tell you that she had gone fishing the night before, you could bet your last dollar that within nine months there would be a new addition to your family.

We all learned to trust her intuition, and on the few occasions when some of us didn't, we always hoped that her prayerful interventions would protect us from our own indiscretions. We knew that Mama Nettie was always praying for us because we were all included on her prayer list. She never started a new day, or went to sleep at night, without praising God for His blessings, and asking Him to take care of everything and everyone on her list.

Her requests were never frivolous. She asked for things like a new roof for the church, relief from asthma for Uncle Charles, and protection for us as we rode down the highway in the rickety, old school bus.

Everything that my grandmother did played a significant role in molding my personality. It did not take much for us to figure out that love, humility, and charity were the main virtues of our daily lives.

My Grandfather: Dad

My grandfather was born in Slidell, Louisiana on March 3, 1900. Dad's name was Charles Rouselle Giles. He was six feet tall with wavy, brown hair, and he always wore a stocking cap at night to hold his hair in place. His mustache was trimmed down short, and when I was older, it would remind me of the one worn by Adolph Hitler. Dad had a long, prominent nose, and a sprinkle of freckles were scattered across his cheeks. His upper incisors were on a removable bridge, and he would delight us by pushing the bridge forward with his tongue.

We would squeal and pretend to be afraid of the menacing teeth, and Dad would grab us and snap at our cheeks. He always called us "scamps," and he had a wonderful sense of humor. He had rheumatoid arthritis, and as the years passed, his hands became so gnarled that he could barely use them.

By the time that Art and I were born, Dad had no family left except for one acquired uncle in Slidell, and one sister who lived in California. Dad never spoke of anyone except his sister, Valerie, and that was usually in his prayers at the dinner table. "Bless my sister in a distant land," he prayed. I thought that California was as far away as China.

My grandfather was named after his father, who had died by the time he was five years old. Dad's mother, Juliette Hamerick died a couple of years after her husband, so her sister Zella, and her husband, Joe Lawrence, of Slidell, Louisiana took him in and raised him. Slidell is located just 16 miles from Pearlington, Mississippi on the Louisiana side of the Pearl River.

When Art and I were still very small, Dad took us to Slidell at least once a week to visit Uncle Joe. Aunt Zella was already dead by then, and Uncle Joe lived in the big house by himself. Slidell had a big Creole and American Indian population, and Dad told us that he was Creole because his ancestors were of French and African descent. When we were growing up in the house, he always spoke French to us, and he spoke French with Uncle Joe, too.

Dad and Uncle Joe always sat in the long, dark kitchen sipping the strong, black brew of coffee and chicory and talking, while Art and I ate giant, purple figs straight from the enormous trees in the yard.

The figs were so succulent and sweet. I would pluck a fig from the branch and gaze at the white droplet of sticky milk that bled from the stem. Mama Nettie used that white sap from the fig stems to heal skin infections like ringworm. I can still taste the honey-sweet flavor of those big figs.

Dad's sister, Aunt Valerie, was a prim and proper old stuffed shirt. She would come from California to visit her brother at Christmas, or for a week or two during the summer months. No matter what we did to prepare things to make the old house clean and comfortable for her, she always had negative things to say about my grandmother's housekeeping. She never said them directly to her, but she always told my Aunt Myrtle or Mama. I guess that was her way of making sure that the message got back to my grandmother.

Dad always managed to tactfully keep the peace between his sister and his wife, and he was extra kind to Mama Nettie for weeks after Aunt Valerie's departure. I always saw the pain in my grandmother's eyes, but she never said a bad thing about her sister-in-law. She really lived by the rule that she taught us: "If you can't say something good about someone, say nothing at all."

It was a mystery that no one ever discussed, but somehow Aunt Valerie met and married Mama Nettie's first husband, Peter Daniels, and they had two children, Monroe and Gloria. Monroe was blind, but both he and his sister were sweet and very loving, and we always enjoyed a visit from them.

Whenever we got news of an imminent visit from Aunt Valerie, doom and gloom fell over my grandmother and me. We did what we could to keep our feelings hidden because we knew how excited Dad was to see his sister. Mama Nettie put the best linens on the bed, and cooked the best meals. We kids did our chores, and stayed as quiet and as out of sight as we could until things were back to normal.

I'll never forget her last visit. Aunt Valerie actually told my mother that she wanted to hose down the walls. That was really cruel. Dad had just paneled the living and dining rooms with those sheets of fake wood. The floor was tiled with burgundy-colored vinyl tile, to match the burgundy leather couch and arm chairs.

The living room was large and uncluttered. There was a coffee table; two matching end tables on either side of the couch; another table with a reading lamp sat next to the chair; an upright piano and its stool sat in one corner; and there were two tall, wooden bookcases that housed an impressive collection of Harvard Classics and a full set of the *Encyclopedia Britannica.*

I just couldn't understand why my great-aunt was so disagreeable. Aunt Valerie's visits were the only dark spots in our otherwise carefree lives.

My grandfather spent a lot of time with us. He taught us how to plant the gardens, and to help him care for the little farm. Our mornings were busy, and after lunch it was nice to take a nap on the back porch. Dad went out in the afternoons to care for the animals, and we had time to go off on our ventures in the woods or just play around the yard.

On the few occasions that we got out of hand, Dad would give us a stern look or a short sermon, but he left the corporal punishment up to my grandmother. We always knew when something was not quite right, because Dad would start humming the same note over and over from some ancient spiritual.

Chapter II

The Beginning

❀❀❀

My Roots

My maternal grandmother, Arnette, told me that the Giles Family lived in Pearlington, Mississippi from 1920 through 1937. My mother's oldest brother, Eugene, whom everyone called Gene, rode on the 4:00 a.m. mail truck from Pearlington every morning to attend school in Bay St. Louis. In 1938, they relocated to Biloxi, Mississippi, because my grandfather found work for a while at the oyster factory. Afterwards, they moved to New Orleans, Louisiana in 1941, where my grandfather worked at the munitions factory during World War II.

Uncle Gene joined the U. S. Army in 1941, and went off to fight in the South Pacific Islands. He returned to the United States in 1945, and was transferred to Camp

Lee, Virginia, where he was discharged from the Army on October 16, 1945.

After returning home to New Orleans, Uncle Gene began working for the United States Post Office on October 25, 1945, just nine days after his discharge from the Army. He remained there for 40 years. In 1947, he joined the Tulane Memorial Baptist Church. He served in many capacities at his church over a 50-year period as: Sunday School Teacher, Secretary for the Board of Trustees, Treasurer of the Church, Chairman of the Deacon Board, Director of the Male Chorus, and President of the Sanctuary Choir.

Uncle Gene had a brief relationship with a beautiful, young woman named Phyllis from New Orleans, and from that union their daughter, Janice, was born on January 25, 1948.

On November 6, 1954, he married Rosie Lee Evans. They had three children: Ava, Arnette, and Eugene, Jr.

In 1959, Uncle Gene joined the National Baptist Convention and served as Secretary of the National Brotherhood Union. Over a 45-year period, he served as their Third Vice President, Second Vice President, and First Vice President. He presided as President over the National Baptist Brotherhood Union from 2000 through 2004.

Uncle Gene kept fit and active by planting a small winter and summer garden. He did lawn work every Thursday, and stayed busy with his church activities. At 82 years old, he still looked like a man of 50.

In 2005, he lost his home to the floodwaters of Hurricane Katrina. He stayed in one of those FEMA trailers with my Aunt Rosie and their son until the house was ready, and finally, they were able to move back home in October of 2007.

In January 2008, just a few months after returning home, the worst imaginable tragedy struck. Aunt Rosie found their son dead in his bed. Eugene, Jr., lovingly known as Brother to everyone, had succumbed to a life-long illness.

As an ever-faithful servant, my uncle never refused a request, and when his pastor asked him to speak at a funeral one scorching day on August 14, 2008, he did not hesitate. Unfortunately, when he reached the church parking lot he felt ill. He exited the car and had a massive stroke as he leaned on the hot hood of the car for support. Uncle Gene was found later and rushed to the hospital. He underwent many treatments to help him recover, and though he made some miraculous strides over the course of more than a year, he was physically weak, and ready to go home. Eugene Maceo Giles passed one day after his 87th birthday, on November 13, 2009.

Back in 1946, the Giles family lived on Iberville Street near downtown New Orleans. My father's older sister, Thelma, lived nearby on South Galvez Street, and my father's parents lived at 316 South Roman Street. It was there in the downtown neighborhood that my mother met my father, Wilfred N. Clementin. Mama was only 16, and Daddy was 20. My father served in France during World War II, and like my Uncle Gene, he was one of the fortunate ones to come home physically unscarred.

Daddy cut a handsome figure when he took Mama to her junior prom at Booker T. Washington High School. I guess Mama really fell hard for that army uniform, and my grandfather made sure that the shotgun was well oiled for a quick wedding.

Mama moved in with her sister-in-law, Thelma, after the wedding, and my grandparents returned to Pearlington, Mississippi. Uncle Gene and his younger brother, Charles, remained in the house on Iberville Street. However, before my grandparents left town, Mama Nettie went to the local corner store to request an open account for her baby daughter.

"Give Shirley anything she needs and I'll come by once a month to take care of the bill," Mama Nettie said.

Sure enough, the following month, Mama Nettie took the bus to New Orleans to visit her daughter, and she stopped in at the store to pay my mother's bill.

"Good morning Mrs. Radasta. I came to pay my daughter's bill."

"Just a minute Nettie," replied Mrs. Radasta in her heavy Italian accent. She turned to a shelf behind the counter, and grabbed a cigar box. "Here you are, it's $147.63."

"How much?" asked Mama Nettie with a gasp.

"The bill comes to $147.63."

"My Lord, what on earth did she buy in one month?"

"I have it all here Nettie. Most of the charges were for red wine, and fruitcakes."

That was a lot of money for my grandmother. She had no idea that the bill would be this much. She had cleaned out the money she had saved up for that rainy day, and just by chance, she had $150.00 in her purse. Her plan was to take Mama shopping to buy whatever she needed for my layette, and leave some cash with her. *I'll have to make some sacrifices,* she thought, but without hesitation she opened her purse and paid the entire bill.

"I'd appreciate it if you would close the account today," Mama Nettie said, and with that she left the store.

Mama Nettie went to visit her daughter. "In the name of Jesus, how in the world could you have possibly consumed $147.63 in one month? I pulled out everything that I had saved up to buy things for the baby, and leave you with something to get by, but it's all gone now. I closed the account at the store, so you'll have to fend for yourself from now on."

I was born just two days after my mother's seventeenth birthday, in January 1947. Mama had remained in labor for three days before they decided to send word to her mother. When my grandmother got to the house, she yelled at my father, "My goodness, man. It's blowing up a gale out there, and you haven't taken my daughter to the hospital yet!"

The streets of New Orleans were flooded, and they had to carry my mother to a taxi to travel the few short blocks to Charity Hospital.

With a consistent diet of red wine and fruitcake, I was probably too hung over to come out on my own, so the issue was forced by a cesarean section. I made my entrance into the world at 8:32 p.m. on January 20, 1947.

When I was three months old, my parents headed west and moved to Berkley, California. My brother, Art, was born nine months later on January 29, 1948, at Alameda Hospital in Oakland, California.

We lived in a little house on a hill in Berkley. Though I was only a baby, I can still remember sights and sounds of the house. There was a steep stairway outside the kitchen door, and I remember how frightened I was whenever we descended it. I remember, too, the sound of clinking milk bottles as the milkman delivered fresh milk every morning.

There were yellow, ruffled, sheer curtains at the windows, and the afternoon sun would stream down on the hardwood floors where I spent most of my time. Art had an old-fashioned buggy. I was too tiny to push it, but I would fix my little body under the frame between the wheels, and crawl across the room until the buggy hit the wall. Then, I'd turn around, and push him until we hit the opposite wall. I called my little brother, "Wootie Wootie," and to my brother's displeasure, that name stuck for quite a few years.

We had one of those old hand-turned movie projectors with the large reels. A big, hot light bulb glared through a lens to transpose the images from the camera to a white sheet that Mama hung on the bedroom door. We would sit and watch the silent, animated wonders of: Andy Panda, Woody Woodpecker and Mickey Mouse, and we continued to watch those movies until the celluloid film cracked and crumbled.

Daddy went to work at the post office, and Mama stayed home and took care of us. Mama was used to having her way, and like her grandmother, Adelaide, she was probably too young to be a wife or a mother. Whatever the case, things didn't work out.

My parents divorced when I was about two-and-a-half, and Mama left Daddy in Berkley, California and moved back to the South with us. She took Art and me to Pearlington, Mississippi to live with our maternal grandparents: Mama Nettie and Dad. I would not recall seeing my father again until I was nearly 14 years old.

When I was about five years old, I remember that a handsome stranger came to visit us. My grandmother let him lie down on the chaise lounge in her bedroom. While he was sleeping, my cousin, Janice, and I crept into the room to get a good look at him. We stood across the room, and I told Janice, "He's so pretty, I want to kiss him."

"Go ahead, give him a kiss," she said. Janice tugged at my hand, and we made a couple of steps towards the sleeping man.

"No, I'm afraid to." We giggled, and backed out of the room.

For years I would hold the image of that man in my mind, and I fantasized that my Prince Charming would certainly look like him. I could never understand why my heart felt so strange, so tender whenever I thought of him. I would not realize that the stranger had been my father until I saw him many years later. He was the first man that I had ever loved. I can remember being ashamed to look into his eyes when we did meet again, for fear that someone would perceive my ignorance and guilt.

When we were old enough to understand, Mama Nettie told us that our mother had to work, and there was no work in Pearlington for her, so she moved 18 miles away to Bay St. Louis. My grandmother just wanted to be certain that we did not feel abandoned by our mother.

Art and I were always excited whenever Mama walked through the doorway to visit us. She only came about once a month, and she was always loaded down with gifts for us. Mama always made beautiful dresses for me to match the ones that she made for herself. Her shiny, dark hair hung well past her shoulders, and she was beautiful with the flamboyant hats that she made to match her dresses.

We were always excited about every aspect of our tiny, little lives. I was excited to see the vegetables that we'd planted grow; excited to see the flowers in bloom; excited to chase the chickens around the yard; excited to pull up a big, greasy alligator garfish from the pier down by the Pearl River, and I was excited to dress up on Sundays for church in soft, chiffon dresses.

Though we loved our mother, and our father, who was absent from our lives, we would never love anyone more than we loved Mama Nettie and Dad. They did everything for us, and they always made me feel safe, secure, and loved.

For a brief period, just before my 30th birthday, my parents got back together, but the rekindled romance lasted for only six months. By then, I was married with four children of my own, so I didn't have much time to play family with my folks. Daddy returned to California after the second breakup, and he remained there until his death on January 19, 1999.

I did not see my father again for 21 more years, but in October of 1998 I took a trip to California to pay him a visit. He was bedridden and had been sick for a few months. We had telephoned each other twice a week for over a year, and though I could never get any real insight as to who he really was, I felt close to him for the first time.

His death came as a shock because I had spoken to him the morning before, and he told me that he was being discharged from the hospital the following day. The doctors had finally determined the source of his illness. After a kidney biopsy, he was diagnosed with an auto-immune disease that attacks vital organs. On the morning of his discharge, however, he woke up with breathing difficulties, and the doctors decided to intubate him. They sedated my father before inserting the tube into his airway, but unfortunately, he never woke up from the anesthesia.

My father was cremated the very next day. I was taken aback for a moment, because I didn't get to see him one last time. By then, though, I had reached a new level of maturity. I realized that our bodies are only a temporary shell, but our spirits are eternal.

Since my father was a World War II Veteran, his family held his ashes in an urn while they awaited a gravesite in a military cemetery. His remains were finally buried on December 14, 1999, in the San Joaquin Valley National Cemetery in southern California.

While waiting for that final resting place, Daddy had sat in his urn atop the television at my stepsister's house for nearly a year. During that period, her TV kept going on by itself.

This strange phenomenon was not limited to her home. On the trip down from Oakland, California to the cemetery, my stepsister, Lorna, and her mother stopped over for the night at a friend's house. They sat Daddy's urn on the mantle in the living room, and sure enough, he turned the television on there, too. I still wonder what message Daddy tried to send them. I think I would have kept Daddy around a bit longer, just to find out.

Chapter III

The Rest of My Family

A New Start

Mama Nettie and Dad met in Slidell, Louisiana shortly after she left Mobile and returned to Mississippi. They courted for a brief period before Dad popped the question and they were married on November 23, 1920.

After the wedding, Dad moved to Pearlington. Mama Nettie and her baby daughter, Myrtle, already lived with Papa Phillip and Phillip, Junior. Young Phillip was very ill, and eventually became bedridden. Mama Nettie and Papa Phillip cared for him until he died in 1922. He was only 18.

"We never knew what was wrong with him," Mama Nettie told me. "Medicine wasn't that refined back then, but he must have had a bowel obstruction because everything came up through his mouth, and the flesh fell away from his hip bone. The doctors didn't have a clue or a cure, so Papa and I did the best that we could to care for him until he passed."

After the loss of his son, Papa Phillip's health began to deteriorate, too. He had never completely recovered from the weeks of exposure while floating in the Gulf of Mexico after a shipwreck in October 1893. Gradually, his weak heart began to fail, and he spent most of his time sitting in the shade of the big oak tree in the front yard.

Dad continued to work at the brickyard in St. Joseph, Louisiana, just north of Slidell. He was up at four o'clock every morning to catch the mail boat, and Mama Nettie got up with him to pack a hearty lunch of beans and biscuits in his metal lunch pail. On Sundays, they made the long walk down the road for church services at Holmes Chapel Methodist Church. Holmes Chapel had opened in 1870 as a Methodist Episcopal Church, and during the early years, it was one of the most prominent churches on the Mississippi Coast.

On November 12, 1922, Mama Nettie gave birth to their first son, Eugene, and their second son, Charles, was born on January 16, 1925.

Dad lost his job at the brickyard, and he did odd jobs around town and planted a garden to keep the family well fed during the Great Depression. He went to hunt in the woods with his two small sons, and he was accidentally shot in the leg during one of those outings in the winter of 1929. Dad was still in the hospital when my mother was born on January 18, 1930, and they named her Shirley Thelma.

Papa Phillip did what he could to help my grandmother around the house while Dad was hospitalized for long periods of time. The young children were able to help her water and weed the small garden. Papa even watched over the four small children when Mama Nettie was forced to take a live-in job for a while, but eventually his weak heart just gave out, and he died in 1934.

My grandparents remained in Pearlington until 1937. They moved to Biloxi and from Biloxi to New Orleans. They were absent from Pearlington for nearly 10 years, and when they returned in 1946 the old homestead had been seized for back taxes. My grandmother found a nice little house situated in the heart of town, and they purchased it for $450.

ETIENNE WILLIAM MAXSON

Uncle Bud and the Ancestors

My great-grandmother Adelaide's brother, Etienne William Maxson, had a house in Pearlington, just across the street from my grandparents on the corner of Whites Road and Hancock Street. We all called him Uncle Bud.

Uncle Bud was retired, but he had earned an impressive work history: He was appointed Deputy Collector of Internal Revenue at New Orleans and served from 1891 through 1892. He was next appointed Commissioner of Elections of Hancock County, Mississippi, and served for two years from 1892-1894. He worked as Manager and Commissioner of Elections representing the Republican Party and served in the county and state as a delegate. On December 6, 1898, he was appointed Postmaster of Pearlington, and served there from January 3, 1899 to May 31, 1916.

Uncle Bud was removed from office under President Wilson's Administration, and was re-employed under the same administration as a war worker in the Air Service Bureau of the War Department at Washington, D.C. After World War I, he was transferred to the Department of Agriculture. He was appointed Census Enumerator for the District of Columbia in December 1919, and he conducted the census during his annual leave in January of 1920. He served under Presidents Harrison, McKinley, Roosevelt, Taft, Wilson, Harding, Coolidge and Hoover over a 30-year period.

Bud was a short, thick man, with green eyes and a rim of white hair. We kids didn't understand anything about race. We knew that some of our folks were dark-skinned, and others light-complexioned. Uncle Bud and Mama Adelaide were both white with straight hair. Color never mattered to us, and Mama Nettie taught us to love all of God's children. We grew up knowing that a person's worth would not be determined by their skin color.

No matter when we went to Uncle Bud's house, he was always seated at his roll-top desk with pen in hand. He had an impressive library of books. Mama Nettie inherited his collection of Harvard Classics after his death in 1957, and I spent many of my summers enjoying them.

Uncle Bud always wore a green sun visor on his nearly bald head when he was indoors. Whenever he went out, he wore a straw hat. Every day, he dressed in a long-sleeved white shirt and tie, and he wore black armbands on his sleeves. When he left the house, or went to the First Baptist Church on Sundays, he wore one of his seersucker suits with the tiny pin stripes.

Art and I went to visit Uncle Bud a couple of days every week. He was already in his late 80s by then. Uncle Bud lived with his wife, Della Frances Moore. She had been ill for a long time and could no longer get out of bed. If we asked Uncle Bud what was wrong with her, he would simply reply that she had the "big sickness."

Aunt Della's pale, ghostly figure seemed long and thin as she lay in the huge bed, dressed in soft, white gowns. She loved to see us, and when Uncle Bud escorted us to the side of her bed, she would stretch her bony, alabaster hand out to pat our cheeks. She could barely speak, but she always gave us a big smile, and then Uncle Bud would quietly lead us away.

Uncle Bud kept a small, gold brocade box in a drawer across from Aunt Della's bed, and when our brief visit with Aunt Della was done, we would beg him to show us the special treasure.

"Can we see the box now Uncle Bud?" I would ask, and he would walk us over to the bureau. He pulled the drawer open and removed the box. We always stood in awe as he exhibited the fine silky mass of Aunt Della's snowy, white hair.

"Go ahead, touch it if you like," he said.

I would run my inquisitive index finger along the soft locks, and then Uncle Bud would withdraw the box and reverently return it to its sacred resting place.

Between 1930 and 1950, Uncle Bud wrote a book called ***The Progress of the Races.*** The book is rich in the history of Pearlington and principal towns along the mouth of the Pearl River. It also covered the skills and ingenuity of African American people after the abolition of slavery, and the great contributions they made to the area.

I always thought that I had asked enough questions when I was young because I was always so inquisitive. However, I don't ever recall hearing anything about the senior Etienne Maxson's biological mother.

Many Haitian women ventured to Mississippi territory when the white settlers began to inhabit the land along the Pearl River, but they were free women. In all probability, Etienne's mother was a slave, and therefore her son was held as a slave, too. He was 35 years old when he was freed from slavery.

Since Mama Adelaide and Uncle Bud never spoke of their grandmother, I can only assume that she was probably dead long before they could remember anything about her. We heard a lot from our relatives about the lives and works of our Favre ancestors, but no piece of the puzzle quite fits to explain the elder Etienne's maternal ancestry.

Stranger yet was that fact that my great-great-grandfather was not treated as a slave. He was taught to read and write and given responsibilities to account for money.

Uncle Bud said that his father, Etienne, rode the mules to turn the mill of the cotton gin at Favrepoint when he was a boy. Later, he worked as a clerk in his master's store. By then, his master was the son of Onezan Favre, Sr., Theophulus Moody Favre, who was born in July of 1849.

During the Civil War, Etienne was entrusted with transporting and selling the Favre's cotton. He drove the wagons by night and hid during the day to avoid contact with thieves, and he always managed to return home safely with the cash from the sale.

Unfortunately, the early census records did not list the names of many slaves, and I could find neither written nor word of mouth information to confirm any of my theories, regarding my African ancestry.

Etienne Maxson and Harriet Garden were obviously married while he was still a slave, because their first child, Isadora, was born in 1858. The United States Census of 1870 listed Etienne, his wife, and all six of their children as mulattos. Uncle Bud was only five years old then, and he had five other siblings: Isadora, Frances, Mamie, Sylvestor, and Hortense. All six of these children were still alive at the time of their mother's death in 1903.

Uncle Bud and his two sisters: Mamie, and my great grandmother Adelaide, born on March 6, 1882, were the only survivors after 1930, and by the time I was born in 1947, only Bud, and my great-grandmother remained.

The U.S. Census records for 1880 through 1910 continued to list all of my family members as mulattos. This included my great-great-grandmother, Harriet, who was absolutely known to be a full-blooded Choctaw. However, by the time the 1930 census rolled around, all of my family members were listed as black folks.

Uncle Bud wrote that his father, Etienne Maxson, was born in 1830, but he never alluded to the fact in his book that the elder Maxson's biological father was a member of the Favre Clan. Etienne's father was one of the sons of the French settler, Simon Favre. Naturally, I found no records to confirm this fact, and everything I know on this subject is strictly by word of mouth.

Simon Favre, the head of the family, was born on May 31, 1760. He met Celeste Rochon in Mobile, Alabama. They were married on March 25, 1801, and they had five children.

Simon was well educated and he spoke the languages of many Native American Tribes. Sometime around 1804, he received a request for help from the Governor of Louisiana, and he left Mobile and headed to wild territory that would eventually become the Pearlington area.

The Mississippi Territory was created in 1798, and the coastal area known as "The Panhandle" was still part of Spanish West Florida. The southern part of Mississippi, which includes Hancock County, did not actually become part of the State of Mississippi until 1813.

Simon Favre was probably the first white man to settle in the Gulf Coastal Region of Mississippi territory, and later his brother, Onezan, followed him to the new land. Their father, Jean Claude Favre, had acquired large portions of land in Mobile, Alabama; Hancock County, Mississippi; and St. Tammany Parish, Louisiana through a British Patent dated April 10, 1771. Jean Claude gave his son, Simon, some property along the Pearl River that stretched from what later became known as Pearlington to the town of Napoleon, Mississippi.

Spanish West Florida records show that in 1804, Simon Favre owned two plantations, which he inherited from his father. Each plantation contained 1,200 arpents. The French used an arpent as a measurement for a unit of land, and the arpent is equal to about 0.85 acres. One plantation was located on the west side of the Little Pearl River, and the other was located on the east side of the Large Pearl River. The name Favrepoint was given to a corner of the northwestern part of Pearlington. As more white settlers moved into the area and began to cultivate the land, the

Favre family built a cotton gin at Favrepoint, and ginned the cotton for all of the farms along the river.

Simon was commissioned by William C.C. Claiborne, who served as the governor of the Territory of Orleans between 1803-1812. Settlers along the Louisiana borders of the Pearl River were pestered by bands of Indians. In an act of desperation, they requested that the governor send Simon Favre to speak to the Indian leaders to ensure the peace. However, once Simon reached his destination in Mississippi, he was arrested, and imprisoned by the resident U.S. Government Indian Agent.

Governor Claiborne sent a letter to Governor David Holmes of Mississippi, dated September 29, 1812, and requested a speedy release of his emissary. There does not appear to be any more records of Simon's activities after this date, and it is assumed that he died some ten months later on July 21, 1813. According to his will, dated May 18, 1812, Simon Favre owned 4,000 acres of land.

Simon's grandson, Theophulus Favre, nicknamed "Oph" and pronounced "Off," was a partner in the mercantile department of the Poitevent & Favre Lumber Company, and he ran his own turpentine business. He was the Representative of Hancock County in the Mississippi Legislature during the 1870s, and he served as Collector of Customs at Bay St. Louis under President Cleveland.

No doubt, Uncle Bud inherited his zeal for politics from his Favre ancestor. The fact that he was an educated, fair-skinned mulatto probably contributed to his political success during that period of change after Reconstruction.

In the old days, Theophulus and his brother, Captain John Favre, ran a prosperous lumber business, and they were said to be Simon's most prominent heirs. The Poitevent & Favre Lumber Company was instrumental in providing the lumber to the northern railroads for the construction of railroad lines.

President Lincoln issued the Emancipation Proclamation on January 1, 1863. However, Missouri, Tennessee and finally Mississippi did not pass their emancipation laws until two years later. Etienne was freed from slavery after November 24, 1865. By then, my great-great-grandfather was a master carpenter, and he earned his first salary as a free man when he built a schooner for Captain John Favre and Captain Mars.

Prior to President Lincoln's Emancipation Proclamation, railroads stopped abruptly at the Mason-Dixon Line, because southerners feared that their slaves would attempt escape if the train lines crossed their borders.

The 244-mile boundary of the Mason-Dixon Line was named for two British surveyors named Charles Mason and Jeremiah Dixon. It took Mason and Dixon four years to complete the survey to settle a land dispute between the owners of Pennsylvania and Maryland. The survey line ran from the southwest corner of Delaware, north to Pennsylvania and west to approximately the southwest corner of Pennsylvania. Although the Mason-Dixon Line was surveyed 100 years prior to the American Civil War, it was later considered to be the divider between the northern and the southern states.

Uncle Bud also failed to mention in his book that his mother, Harriet Garden, was a full-blooded Choctaw Indian. All that we know through word of mouth about Harriet is that her father was a Choctaw chief. She was born in 1840 and lived to be about 63 years old. Property records at the Hancock County Tax Office in Bay St. Louis, Mississippi show that her land was conveyed to her children after her death. The date of the deed transfer was August 11, 1903, so Harriet probably died in January or February of that year.

I learned through my research that the Choctaws let some blacks become part of their nation by allowing them to become tribal members. This fact would probably provide an explanation as to how it was possible for my great-great-grandmother, the daughter of a Choctaw chief, to marry a mulatto slave.

While searching through land records, I discovered that my great-grandmother Adelaide was excluded from her mother's last will. Harriet left her property to all of her children except her youngest daughter, Adelaide. Perhaps she had made this exclusion because Adelaide was already a property owner. The Favre family had given her a lovely piece of land situated on the Pearlington-Logtown border.

The U.S. Government did everything it could to remove the Native Americans from the face of the earth in order to take their land. It established the General Allotment Act of 1887. Under the act, tribal lands were allotted to individuals who swore to separate themselves from any Indian tribes, and to live as a "civilized" citizen of the United States.

The Dawes Commission was established in 1893 to negotiate a land allotment agreement that would establish individual rights to land for members of the Five Civilized Tribes which included: the Cherokee, Chickasaws, Choctaw, Muskogee Federation (Creek) and Seminole.

The Muskogee (Creek) Indians held land primarily in Georgia and Alabama, and they had a confederacy made up of the Tallahassee, Atossee and Alibamos Tribes. In 1812, they were armed to fight to protect their land. However, General Andrew Jackson delivered the final massacre to the Creeks on March 27, 1814.

In 1830, Choctaw Chief Chikla moved to an area called Devil's Swamp, which is located across Highway 90 southeast of Pearlington. The small Devil's Swamp Band of Choctaws remained in the swamp until it was safe for them to venture out. Eventually, the women and children would make the daily walk of over 16 miles to Bay St. Louis, where they sold their woven baskets.

During the relocation of the Choctaws to the territory that is now Oklahoma, many Mississippi Choctaws refused to leave their homeland, but nearly all of the Choctaws had left Pearlington by 1902. Like my relatives, many of the Choctaws who could get by just mingled in with the population.

In 1903, the U.S. Government's Dawes Commission reported approximately 2,700 Mississippi Choctaws, most of whom were located along the Pearl River in the north central part of Mississippi. By 1910, the number had dropped to 1,253. Many had died off from influenza and other epidemics that were passed on by the "civilized" invaders. However, the census numbers were not very accurate, because like my relatives, many Choctaws refused to be counted in the census for fear that they would be forced to leave their land.

My great-great-grandmother Harriett was obviously happy to give up her title as Choctaw Princess. It's not difficult to understand why so many of the Indian population would choose to relinquish their language, customs, and traditions to remain in the land of their fathers.

The laws of that time stated that the race of a child should be determined by the race of the mother, but obviously, everyone took great efforts to make certain that the Choctaw ancestry was removed from our family lineage.

There was great hope for the advancement of blacks when the long suffering and injustice of slavery drew to an end. During that awful period of persecution to the American Indians, being black must certainly have seemed like a sure ticket to success.

I was raised as a little black girl on the Mississippi Gulf Coast, but I never quite felt that I belonged to any one race. That underlying feeling was probably prompted by some genetic outcry, for even without my knowledge, I was part Choctaw, part African, part French and part Italian. Why must humans be labeled, anyway? I am so thankful to God that I was born. I don't blame or begrudge anyone for what they are. I am a child of God, and an heir to His kingdom.

When I resided in Italy, I really did love my sojourn there. There are very fair-skinned Italians with a Nordic mixture, and there are dark Italians with a Moorish or Arabic mixture. However, they are all Italians. Color is only used to distinguish one's skin tone, and I enjoyed being called "La bella mora," which means, "The beautiful dark one."

When I returned to America towards the end of 1996, I fell on my knees to praise God that I had removed my children to a neutral environment where they were able to grow without racial prejudices.

Uncle Bud had very emphatic ideas about segregation of the races. He voiced his opinion in an appendix of his book called "Why are There Different Colors of the Human Race?" He was all for equality for all people. However, he did not believe that it was in God's great plan for the races to mix.

When I was old enough to understand, it made me very sad to think that my uncle may have despised his own flesh because he had mixed genes. Had he struggled throughout his life, wishing that God had blessed him with racial purity?

Uncle Bud did finally acknowledge his Choctaw heritage in 1946, when he and Mama Adelaide went down to Gulfport, Mississippi to file a claim to receive their portion of the restitution to the Choctaws as their mother's rightful heirs. Thousands of people, from all walks of life, flocked to make a claim, but disgruntled government workers threw out most of the claims, and my folks never received anything.

My Paternal Grandparents

My paternal grandmother, Stella Suberville, was born on May 2, 1892, in New Orleans, Louisiana. My grandfather, Arthur Clementin was born on April 17, 1887. We called my grandmother, Da, and my grandfather, Paw. Daddy was the baby of the family, and he had two sisters named Thelma and Louise, and two brothers named Louis and Arthur Jr.

When I turned seven years old, Mama Nettie put Art and me on the Greyhound Bus at Pearlington, and Da met us at the bus depot in New Orleans. Though we were only 26 miles from downtown New Orleans, Pearlington seemed light years away.

There were four other members living in their household: Da's mother, Mary Watkins, Aunt Louise and her two sons, Allen and Ronald. Aunt Louise was married to a Turkish man named Mohammed Alley. Unfortunately, they didn't get along well, and they were separated. Divorce was never an option because the Clementins were all good Catholics. Mohammed was always around, though. He loved his sons and took good care of them. They attended the best schools and always wore the best shoes and clothes.

Da always did what she could to make certain that Art and I never forgot that we were a part of the Clementin family. She sent us cards on holidays and our birthdays. She sent money for my first pair of skates, and she paid for a shiny new bike on my 11th birthday.

It was there at Da and Paw's house that I first saw my father, his new wife, and two children: Lorna and Renee'. The year was 1961, and it was then that I realized that my Prince Charming was actually my father. He was white with a head of straight, black hair. He appeared tall when I was five, but now, he only stood a head taller than me.

I wish that there was more to say about this side of my family. I only knew that my grandmother spent most of her days in the kitchen, cooking lots of food, and she wore a small black doily on her head when she attended Mass. Paw worked at a bank, and passed the collection basket at St. Joseph's Church on Tulane Avenue every Sunday. When he was home, he was usually yelling for my grand-mother to do something for him. They didn't appear to be happy or loving like my other grandparents, so I always thought that they were rather odd folks.

Chapter IV

My Mother

Mama

My mother, Shirley, was born on January 18, 1930, and she was the youngest of four children. Mama's older sister, my Aunt Myrtle, was just a little more than a year old when Mama Nettie and Dad were married, so she grew up as a Giles and never knew any other father. Mama's other siblings were named: Eugene (Gene), born on November 12, 1922, and Charles, born on January 16, 1925.

When Mama was only three years old, she sat down at the piano and began playing the jumping beats of the 1930s. Music would be a sacred part of her entire life from that day on. Wherever we lived, there was always an old piano, and no matter how dismal the house may have been,

Mama would cheer things up with her music. Even when it was time to wax the hardwood floors, she managed to make the job fun for us. Mama sat at the piano playing while she sipped pink champagne, and my sister, Faith and I would glide across the floor on polishing rags like professional ice skaters.

Papa Phillip and Myrtle cared for the baby most of the time when Mama Nettie had to leave her children to go out to work. Her two older brothers spoiled her rotten. Mama always trailed her brother, Charles, around and their favorite hiding place was under the raised house.

One day while they were playing, they spied a bottle sitting on one of the thick wooden sills of the foundation. Uncle Charles reached up to retrieve the bottle from its hiding place. He unscrewed the top and took a sniff of its clear contents. He stuck his tongue to the bottle to taste the liquid.

Mama tugged at his sleeve. "Want some," she chided.

Charles put the bottle to the baby's lips, and he laughed at the face she made when the strange taste hit her tongue.

"Ha, ha! This must be Papa Phillip's corn liquor. Here, have another taste," he said.

Uncle Charles and Mama sat under the house, sipping and giggling until they had consumed a good quantity of the bottle's contents. "We better fix this bottle so Papa won't know that we've been in it," Charles said. They replaced the missing liquor with water from the pump and put the bottle back in its original hiding place under the house.

Unfortunately, that was the beginning of their drinking addiction. The two siblings would never lose their taste for alcohol, and it would be the one thing that would eventually destroy both their lives.

Mama had so many talents. Years later when she started nursing for a living, she often took a sabbatical from the hospital and worked by playing music with local bands along the Gulf Coast. She could draw, too, and she painted wall murals when she needed to get a break from caring for sick folks.

She started doing private duty nursing around 1957, and worked in a nursing home, too, for a while. By 1959, my stepfather, Ben, and Mama were both working for a liquor supply company. I never did understand how they managed this, since Prohibition didn't end in Mississippi until around 1966. I guess they must have been bootlegging liquor from another state.

I remember an incident that happened during that period that really frightened me. Mama received a phone call late one night, and I could tell by the sound of her voice that something terrible had happened. Ben and another worker were transporting a large truck full of liquor, and they had been hijacked on the highway. The thieves tied Ben and his colleague to trees in the woods, and stole the truck with its contents. Luckily, they were unharmed, but everyone seemed to be nervous after that, so Mama, and Ben decided to get out of the liquor transport business, and they opened a bar in Waveland, Mississippi. They named the place "The Tropical Inn," and Mama painted large palm trees and beach scenes on the walls of the large room.

Their marriage had been shaky for years, and after they opened the bar, things got much worse. In less than a year after the inauguration of the bar, Mama and Ben decided to split up.

Mama took my sister Faith and me, and we moved in with one of her girl friends.

Mama's lawyer advised that we should not appear to be neglected, for fear that it would harm her chance of obtaining full custody of Faith. So, we were told not to talk to anyone, and never to leave the house after we got in from school. About a month later, Mama rented an old house in Waveland, Mississippi. Bay St. Louis and Waveland border each other, so we were only about eight miles from our old home. Faith and I rode the school bus to Bay St. Louis to continue grade school at St. Rose.

We were in Waveland about six months when Ben came to visit. He told Mama that he was moving to Oklahoma, and he wanted to take his daughter, my sister Faith, with him. Mama agreed to the arrangement and let him take her six-year-old baby, and there I was, totally alone. I had taken care of Faith since her birth. I bathed and fed her, and got her dressed for school. She was more my baby than Mama's, so it was really hard for me to say goodbye.

Mama kept the bar, and continued to run it on her own. Dad was totally devastated about the fact that his daughter was in the bar business. If my grandparents were praying for things to go badly, their prayers were certainly answered. The bar closed down and Mama went back to nursing. She did a lot of private duty home care, and a few years later she started working at Hancock General Hospital in Bay St. Louis.

Around 1967, the hospital asked all nurses to bring in their licensure, and since Mama didn't have one, she resigned and went to nursing school in New Orleans. After graduating, she began working at Slidell Memorial Hospital. Mama was a top nurse who took good care of her patients, and no mess from her doctors. Everyone loved and respected her and her work.

In the early part of the 1970s, my Aunt Myrt sold her old house in Pearlington to Mama, and she purchased a house on several acres of land in the little township of Ansley, Mississippi. Ansley is located across Highway

90, just southeast of Pearlington. There was a barn and a stable for her horses too.

Aunt Myrt worked at Slidell Memorial Hospital as a Nurse's Aide, and she and Mama carpooled. In October of 1980, she telephoned Mama. "Hello, Babe. I'm on my way."

"Okay," Mama replied. "I still have to comb my hair, but I'll be ready to go by the time you get here."

The two sisters hung up, and Aunt Myrt headed out. Though it was two o'clock in the afternoon, the fog was already thick. The dense fog was also mixed with smoke, too. The hunters were in the woods, and they often set fire to the brush. The mixture of smoke and fog proved to be a deadly combination that day.

Aunt Myrt pulled her little Ford pickup truck up on the blacktop road that ran to Highway 90. Just as she entered the first big curve, an 18-wheeler loaded down with steel rods, crossed the yellow line, and plowed her down. The cab of the little truck was crushed, and her life slipped away there on the road.

Within a few minutes, someone knocked on Mama's door to tell her about the accident. "Come on in. We have time for a cup of coffee," Mama yelled. No one responded, and the knocking continued. Mama walked to the back door. The wooden door was open, and the screen door wasn't latched. To her surprise, a young woman from town stood at the door. "Oh, Bernice. I thought you were Myrtle."

"That's why I'm here," Bernice replied. "I'm so sorry Miss Shirley, but your sister is dead."

"You're a liar," Mama replied. "I just spoke to my sister two minutes ago."

"I'm sorry to tell you, but there's been a terrible accident on Ansley Road. She's gone Miss Shirley. She's gone!"

Mama ran to her car, and sped down the road. There were dozens of cars parked along the road, and as she neared the scene of the accident, her heart stopped. No one could have survived that wreck. Aunt Myrt was survived by her husband, Wilhelm James Terrell and their three children: Iris Cleo, Alvin (Brother), and Gay Carol.

Mama was devastated by the death of her sister. They had some differences when she was younger, but they had formed a close relationship, and the two sisters had become best friends.

Like her grandmother, Adelaide, Mama had an intimacy with guns, and she became lovingly known as "Shotgun Shirley." Even though she lived in an isolated spot in the nearly deserted town of Pearlington, no one had the courage to bother my mother or her property. Besides the shotgun, Mama kept a pearl-handled Derringer under her pillow, a .38 Special Smith & Wesson Long Barrel on the nightstand, and a machete under the bed next to her sawed off shotgun.

We always joked that she would pepper an intruder with the shotgun, pull out the .38 and fill them up with six rounds of lead, and grab the machete to chop off their kneecaps. Evidently, that standing joke struck great fear into the hearts of all of the local thieves and would-be troublemakers.

Mama had three hobbies: fishing, cooking and playing the piano. She excelled in all three, and she could catch a mess of fish when no one else could get a bite. Mama would fish in the Gulf, on the Pearl River, in lakes, and freshwater ponds. She would trample through snake-infested swamps with her gun and machete to cut a path to some unknown mud hole. You could rest assured that when she emerged from the woods, her bucket would be filled with fat perch and green trout.

Like her grandmother, Mama also had a way of snaring husbands. Unfortunately, every one of them had the same vice in common. They all drank heavily. Her third and fourth husbands, both Slidell, Louisiana residents, were both heavy drinkers. She divorced number three after a year of something shy of matrimonial bliss. She attempted to divorce husband number four after a couple of years, but he held out for ten years until he finally consented to the divorce.

Mama had a personal, longstanding problem with vodka, and she had consumed enough to cook a few dozen livers. She took an early retirement from nursing around 1985. Shortly afterwards, she married her fifth husband, Sgt. John Merritt. He was working as an Army recruiter in Slidell. After his assignment in Louisiana, they packed up and moved to Seoul, Korea for a tour of duty. Upon returning to the United States, Sgt. Merritt was stationed at Red Stone Arsenal in Huntsville, Alabama. He retired around 1996, and they moved back to Pearlington.

After more than 30 years of heavy drinking, it finally caught up with Mama, and her health began to deteriorate around 1998. Her liver was failing, and she had also gone into kidney failure. She nearly died in Slidell Hospital, but my two daughters, Shaun and Julie, raised much cane until the doctors made the decision to airlift Mama to Chicago.

Mama remained hospitalized at Loyola Hospital for a little over four months. They were finally able to stabilize her, but she required dialysis three times per week, and the doctors placed her on a waiting list for a liver and kidney transplant. After Mama's release, she moved in with my daughter, Julie, who was residing in Racine, Wisconsin.

Racine was only an hour's drive to Loyola Hospital, so that was logistically the best place for her to be.

Mama hated the cold, and the seclusion of being in a place where she had no friends. She missed her husband, and her fishing holes, but the thing that she missed the most was her lifelong companion - vodka. Even on dialysis, she could not resist the desire to drink. We learned that she would pay the Racine taxi drivers to take her from dialysis to the liquor store, and she would hide her bottles under the mattress or in her closet.

One day, Mama declared that she was ready to go home, and despite protests from her doctors, because they wanted her nearby in case the transplant organs become available, she packed her bags and went back to Pearlington. Once at home, she continued her program of dialysis.

In 1989, while at Red Stone Arsenal Army Base, Mom had a right knee replacement, and by 1999, it began giving her trouble. Her knee would swell as big as a basketball. The doctors treated her, but she was in excruciating pain, and nothing helped. When they did decide to take her to surgery they discovered a bleeder, and the knee was too infected to reroute the blood back into her system. Two attempts to stop the bleeding did not work, and before the surgeon took her back to the operating room for a third attempt, he warned us that amputation was a possibility.

Luckily, the third operation was successful. However, they were forced to remove the artificial knee joint, and they fused the knee space with cement. The pain was constant, and she remained immobile for months. The constant swelling and pain forced the doctors to try another procedure after nearly a year of failed treatments. They did another surgery to remove the cement, and placed a steel ball with rods to keep the upper and lower portions of her leg bones together. Mom stayed in a cast and was sent to the rehabilitation section of the hospital for about six weeks.

On the day that Mama was discharged from the hospital, she was being lifted from the wheelchair into the van, and her thighbone snapped at the top of the cast. Mama actually went on home that Friday afternoon, but she was in so much pain that by Monday morning she returned to the hospital. An x-ray of the leg showed the fracture, so poor Mama was taken back to surgery yet another time. An external rod was fixed from her hip to her ankle with long screws that penetrated her flesh, and exited on the opposite side. Due to her illness, and the blood thinners that she took for dialysis, the healing process took nearly a year.

My brother, Art, had retired from his job as a school administrator in Michigan, and moved to nearby Bay St.

Louis, Mississippi. He and his wife, Laverne, took care of Mama every day. Art wanted to take her home with them, but Mama refused to leave her old house in Pearlington. My younger daughter, Shaun, did what she could to help, too.

Mama and her husband had separated, but he was usually around during the day. A visiting nurse and a nurse's aide made rounds throughout the week, and a therapist worked with her because the pin that ran through her ankle had locked her foot into a downward position.

After spending two years with Art in Michigan, I moved to Wisconsin to be near my son, Craig, and daughter, Julie.

I went home a few times in 2001, but after I sustained a fall, and hurt my back in July of that year, I was pretty much out of commission. Eventually, I could no longer work. I called Mom almost daily, and every time I spoke to her, I became more concerned about her condition. When I'd call Art to get the real scoop, I was angry, and saddened to learn that Mama's frequent delirium was the result of a mixture of alcohol and pain medication.

I remember the one and only time that I had ever sassed my mother. I was 21 years old. My son, Craig, was burned when I accidentally spilled hot water under his buttocks while trying to construct a tent to help him through an asthma attack. I immersed him in cold water and rushed him to the hospital. The burn was about an inch wide, and three inches long. Craig was bandaged and lying on his stomach when Mama came by. She had been drinking, and began yelling at me. "I told you to be careful, and now look what you've done to my boy."

I was already nervous, upset, and feeling very guilty for hurting my baby, but Mama wouldn't let me explain that it was an accident, or even how it happened. I looked her in the eyes, and I said, "Stop it, just shut up. You don't know what happened, you're drunk, and you have no right to yell at me."

"What did you say?" Mama glared at me.

"I said that you're drunk, and you're a drunkard. One of these days, the alcohol is going to catch up with you, and I'm not going to be the one to take care of you."

With those words, Mama drew back and slapped me hard across the face.

"Go ahead, and hit me again," I yelled, "It won't change anything, you're still a drunkard."

With that invitation, Mama drew back once again, and gave me another slap.

I never forgot that day. I was raised well, and no matter what, I was supposed to respect my mother. That was the first and last time that I broke the fourth commandment.

Even though Mama was not a pleasant person to be around when she was drinking, I vowed never to disrespect her again.

Now, I had reached a point in my life where I felt that I would have to eat those words. Mama needed me, and even though my heart had softened, I was not physically able to be of much use to a bedridden parent. Besides, everyone knows that former nurses make the worst patients. The fact that she was self-medicating herself beyond safe limits, and still drinking, sent sparks of anger through my veins, and I tried to comprehend what it must be like to be so addicted to a substance.

Due to my poor health, I moved to Florida to live with my son, Jeremy, in October of 2002, and I went to Pearlington to spend the week between Christmas and the New Year of 2003 with Mama. I stretched out on the bed next to her and stroked her hair as she slept. I thought, ***This is Mama Nettie's baby. If she were alive, she would be here taking care of her, as she had taken care of me, my children, and dozens of needy strangers. Could I be so unfeeling?***

When I returned to Florida, I was tormented about the thought of my mother. The old house was crumbling down around her. She barely ate, and she was alone most nights. Art was only 20 minutes away, but he was a man.

My mother still had her pride, and she was struggling to hang on to her dignity. She needed help for toileting and bathing, too. My mother needed me.

I made every excuse in the book to myself. I was afraid of snakes and spiders, and I was convinced that the house would fall down on me. The house was dirty, and humid, and it rained through the roof in the den. There was no place for me to sleep, and no place to put my things. I was in constant pain. I had injured my lower back, and rotated my right hip. I already had a slight curvature of the lumbar spine, and pinched nerves in my neck. I had constant headaches, and a pinched sciatic nerve in my right leg left me literally in pain from head to toe.

One night in February 2003, after only two hours of sleep, I was forced to crawl out of bed. I was kneeling because that position was the most comfortable one for me. I began to pray, "Lord! Thy will be done, but please take me tonight, or heal me." I knelt there praying for hours. I didn't want to endure another day of pain. Finally, I seemed to hear a voice responding to me.

"Go to Pearlington, and I will heal you."

Once again, I prayed the same prayer, and I received the same reply. I began to cry even harder, and I said, "Lord! Ask me anything, but please don't ask me to go to

Pearlington. Mama's still drinking. I can't take her belligerence and sarcasm."

My grandparents and my baby, Shannon, who died at birth, were all buried there. I was living in Pearlington when my husband, Maurice, was killed in an automobile accident on the highway near home. There were too many bad memories, too many ghosts in Pearlington.

No matter how hard I tried to rationalize the issue, the pain got worse, and the voice kept saying the same thing. After another terrible night around the second week of March, I phoned Art and asked if he could come to Florida to get me. I had given up. I was going to Pearlington to take care of Mama. I told him not to tell her. I didn't want her to be disappointed, should I back down at the last minute and change my mind.

The sun was just beginning to set as we pulled down the driveway, and parked on the gravel in the back yard. I grabbed one of my bags from the back seat of Art's van, and walked up the wheelchair ramp. I stopped at the back door for a second and took a deep breath before entering. "Lord, please let this work," I prayed quietly to myself.

Mama was lying in bed, and she pulled herself up on a large metal triangle, which hung inches from her head. A big smile spread across her face, and it pained me to see her missing front teeth. She'd always had a mouthful of beautiful, straight, white teeth. Now, since starting the dialysis, she had begun losing them. Her tiny, slanted eyes pinched together even tighter as the outer edges were forced up by the smiling mechanism of her cheeks.

"Well, how did you manage to sneak up on me? What a surprise!"

Art and his wife, Laverne, were standing behind me, and we all had big grins on our faces. I walked around to the far side of the bed, bent down, put my arms around Mama's neck, and planted a kiss on her cheek. "I've come to take care of you, and to get you up out of this bed if you want me to, and I'll stay as long as you need me," I said.

"My child has come home to take care of me. Why yes! Of course I want you," Mama replied. With that, she pulled my face close to her, and kissed me on the lips.

The doctor had just removed the rod and screws from Mama's leg, and the nurse came several days per week to clean the sixteen screw sites, and apply an antibiotic cream and gauze, to keep the holes infection free.

I settled in the best that I could. I slept in the room with Mama on her old water bed that was pushed to the railing of her hospital bed, and I left my clothes packed in the middle of the floor. I was up early the next day, and I set out to do what I could to make Mama comfortable. She would only eat about two tablespoons of oatmeal for breakfast, and I had to mix it with enough milk to allow her to drink it through a straw.

The State of Mississippi sent out "Meals on Wheels" every week, but Mama refused to eat the pre-packaged food. She was supposed to be on a high-protein diet, but even if I tried to cook fish or meat for her, she would move it around on her plate, and bury it under a slice of bread.

I did the best that I could to give her sponge baths, comb her hair, and help her to get dressed on the days that she went to dialysis. We got up at four o'clock in the morning to have her ready when the medical transport van came by to pick her up at 5:30 a.m. At that time, Mama could navigate on her own enough to slide from the bed to the potty chair, or into her wheelchair.

We would laugh hard while trying to get her into her clothes. I would climb on the bed with her, and try to get her feet into her underpants and slacks. Mama had a stick that helped her grab things, so she would pull, and tug on everything. I could not bend my back because of the pain, so I had to kneel down on the floor in order to get her shoes and socks on.

One Saturday, Mama dismissed her nurse. "Take tomorrow off. You need some time to spend with your family. My daughter can clean and dress my leg for me."

"Are you sure?" the nurse asked.

"Yes, I'm sure. You just go ahead and have a nice day off."

I stood in horror. I was too embarrassed to protest, but Mama knew well that there was no nursing in me. Until I turned nine, I always replied that I wanted to be a nurse if someone asked what I wanted to do when I grew up. Mama was working at the nursing home that year and every morning a group of nurses stopped in at our house for coffee, when they finished their shift. They would all sit around the dining room table discussing their patients. Poor Mr. Cease, was the cancer patient who had to have his skull plate removed, and his oozing brains cleaned on a daily basis.

They talked about the most repulsive conditions. It's no wonder that fifty years later, I still can't stand to eat breakfast. Those early morning conversations turned my stomach and killed my desire to be a nurse. Until I had children, I could not stand the thought of a crippled crab. Afterwards, I was forced to kiss cuts, and bandage scraped knees, but that was for my kids. Now, I had been manipulated into being a nurse, and I wasn't a happy camper.

When Sunday rolled around, I took deep breaths, and prayed that I could get through the job without gagging. When I was done, I turned to Mom and said, "Please don't ask me to do this again." From then on, we left that part of her care up to the nurse. I didn't know it then, but I would be called to do many things that I never even imagined myself capable of achieving.

A physical therapist came every Tuesday and Thursday, to get Mama up out of bed and moving around with the aid of a walker. Initially, she was only able to make about ten steps. I kept pushing her to try to go a few steps more.

"You have to increase your distance if you ever want to regain your strength," I would tell her.

Sometimes, she would become angry and snap at me. "I know what I can do. I don't need anyone to tell me what I can do with my body." The next time, she would double her distance and give me a big smile. "You see, I can do it if I want to."

Around May 2003, Mama started complaining of left shoulder pain. Art and I took her to the orthopedic specialist, and an x-ray showed a torn rotator cuff. Due to the seriousness of her current illness, and the blood thinner medication, corrective surgery was not an option. So, the problem was resolved with increased doses of pain pills.

In June, Mama had some occasional upper right side pain, and one night she began to experience some shortness of breath. I called an ambulance, and we went to the emergency room at Slidell Hospital. She was having some lower gastro-intestinal bleeding, too, so she was hospitalized. Tests showed that she had gallstones, but her physical condition would not support surgery for this either. Her blood platelet count was so low that the doctor refused to scope her to find the source of the GI bleed. Once again, Mama was sent home with more pain pills.

Art and I had tried to learn the truth about Mama's condition from her liver specialist. However, he was always vague and blunt. "Your mother is a very sick lady." That's all that we knew. I was very upset with the doctor's lack of concern, and I scheduled an appointment with the doctors at the dialysis clinic to see if we could get some straight talk from them.

The doctors were very pleasant and informative. We were finally given the real story, and we later learned that most of it had been withheld from us at Mama's request. By this time, Mama began to retain fluid in her abdomen and the left side of her body. Her arm and leg were painfully swollen, and the dialysis was not pulling away the excess fluid. She had a second attack of shortness of breath, and once again I rushed her to the hospital via ambulance. They ran more tests, and after the third day, I received a call from the head physician of the dialysis clinic.

"I have just looked at your mother's latest test results and her liver x-rays. We can do no more for your mother, and the only thing that we are currently doing is prolonging her agony with the dialysis treatments. There is no hope of improving her condition, because her liver and kidneys are gone."

Tears welled up in my eyes, and my words seemed to split my throat. "You mean that she's dying?" I asked.

"I'm very sorry, but there's no hope," the doctor replied. "I feel that the best thing would be for you to make a decision to discontinue the dialysis. At this point, it's just adding to her pain, and it's not helping. Her organs have failed completely."

"If Mama were mentally incapacitated, I would consider your recommendation. However, she has good mental faculties. I will talk to her, but the decision must be hers. She's always had to be in control of her life, and I cannot take away this final act of dignity."

"If you like, I will go to talk to her, too, and if she decides, we will have someone from hospice come in to talk to you all."

"Yes! I would like that. Thank you, doctor," I replied.

I stood there at the pay phone in the hallway of the hospital. A sick feeling spread over me. My knees felt weak, and I wished that there were some place for me to sit. I don't know how long I stood there. I remember picking up the phone to call my two daughters and my brother.

When I returned to Mama's room, I could tell by the look on her face that the doctor had already spoken to her. I sat down beside her and leaned over to put my head on her chest.

"I'm so sorry, Mama," I cried. "I never thought that you were going to die. I came to help you get better."

We stayed like that for a long time, and finally Mama said, "Doctor Baltizar came in, and showed me my liver x-rays. My liver looks like a rice strainer. I know that there's no hope. He was so kind. He sat here and held my hand, and he cried like a baby. I'm going to let them stop the dialysis," she said.

"Are you sure that's what you want, Mama?" I stammered. "You know that this is your decision."

"Yes, I know. There's just no hope. It's too late for the transplants, and it's too late for me. I've had a good life, and now, it's my time to go."

Someone called to tell me that the director of hospice would be in to talk to the family at one-thirty that afternoon. Everything seemed so surreal. Even the light seemed to have changed, and I was still moving and functioning, but I felt as if I was looking through a window into a scene that belonged to someone else.

Everyone was so gentle. The hospice director met with us in a private area outside of Mama's room. She explained all of the services that they would provide, which included daily nursing care, medication and equipment. When she started explaining about the oxygen tanks, the body lift and the suction tubes, she turned to me and held my hand.

"We will show you how to use all the equipment, and—"

With those words, I stopped her in the middle of her sentence, and I withdrew my hand from hers and pressed them both to my face.

"But you don't understand," I replied. "I don't want to know how to use those things. I can't! No, I can't do that to my mother." The tears flowed down my cheeks, and I could feel several hands caressing my shoulders and arms.

I sat there for a long time after everyone had left. I thought about everything that had led up to this point. I thought about my vow more than 35 years earlier: I would not be the one to take care of Mama. I thought about how I had moved 5,000 miles away, and the events that had transpired to lead me back to her. I took a deep breath, and prayed, "Lord, give me the strength to do what I must, because I'm the one. I'm the only one."

I went back to Mama's room and told her about our meeting with Hospice. I sat next to her bed and held her hand. "Well, if this is what you want, I promise that I will stay with you to the end. I will sit by your side, hold your hand, and sing you into glory."

Mama squeezed my hand. "Yes, my baby, that's what I want."

Art and I followed the ambulance as Mama rode home for the last time. We spent the next few days making phone calls to our children and grandchildren, and I had the task of calling Mama's last surviving sibling, Uncle Gene.

Although we all knew that the end was inevitable, the fact that it had arrived was still shocking to everyone. Mama was always so strong. Even in her most fragile moments, she always smiled and hid the pain from everyone. Mama's death would bring on the end of an era. She was the last of the female daredevils. Mama had blazed a trail with her machete and guns. Shotgun Shirley was on her way out.

The hospice nurse warned me that Mama might become agitated as the poisons from her liver and kidneys began to take over her body. I prayed that her rage would not manifest itself. She was nauseous for several hours after we got her settled in her bed. I held a basin on her chest and soothed her brow with a cool cloth. After about four hours, she started to feel better, and I sat holding her hand and singing one of Dad's old hymns.

Without warning, Mama started yelling about some money that she had given to her ex-husband, John. I tried to calm her with a soothing voice, but that had no effect. I don't know where it came from, but finally I opened my mouth.

"Stop it! You stop this ranting, and raving right this minute! You have always manipulated everyone to get what you wanted, but I'm no longer your little, timid girl. You told me that you wanted to come home to die in peace in your own bed, and I promised to hold your hand, and sing you into glory. If that's what you want, that's fine, but your reign as tyrant is over! I'm in charge now, and you're going to do exactly what I tell you. You are going to be peaceful, or I'm going to take you back to the hospital and leave you there. Do you understand me?"

Mama gazed at me through the tiny slits of her eyes, bit her lower lip, and remained silent for a while. Finally, she reached for my hand.

"Well! You are the matriarch now. I guess I better be a good girl."

I stood up from my chair, and then sat down on the bed next to her.

"We'll be just fine," I said, and I bent down and put my arms around her neck, and my head on her chest. "I love you, Mama!"

"My baby, my baby," Mama said, and she caressed my hair until she fell off to sleep.

True to my word, I stayed by Mama's side, and I read her Psalms from Dad's old Bible. We sang hymns together, and I held her hand, and tried to keep my promise to sing her into glory. The most valuable thing that I accomplished was asking Mama if she would like to see the priest. When she said yes, I was overjoyed.

Monsignor Carroll was already retired, but he was temporarily serving at St. Joseph's Church while the parishioners waited for a new priest to be installed. Monsignor came to visit, and he heard Mama's confession. He would return once more to anoint her with the final Sacrament of Extreme Unction, the Last Rites.

Everyone came out to Pearlington to visit Mama, and I spent most of my time at her bedside. Art came up with a great idea to give Mama a going away party. The doctors had advised us that her life expectancy would probably be about three weeks after the final dialysis treatment. We decided that the party should be held while Mama was still relatively strong.

Every living soul in Pearlington brought food, and turned out for the going away party. Mama wanted to get out of bed, and she managed to sit in her wheelchair for four hours. She was happy to see so many of her old friends, and a lot of her old drinking buddies. Her special friends spent a quiet moment with her. They held hands or hugged, and laughed and cried together. It was a mixture of pain and joy to say farewell. The party was a great success, and within two days Mama started her journey home.

My sister, Faith, drove in from Georgia in time for the party, and she stayed at the house with me until Mama passed. She was having a rough time of it, and had stayed away as long as she could. Faith had gone through her father Ben's lengthy illness and death from stomach cancer in 1989, and she was afraid to see Mama deteriorate and die in nearly the same fashion.

When Mama hit the two-week mark, she was no longer alert. She had suffered a seizure and she was losing her ability to swallow. I was told to administer smaller doses of the medication at more frequent intervals, so her doses were changed to every thirty minutes. It was a devastating time for me.

Although I had been obedient to God's order, I was still plagued with back pain and headaches, and even though Art and my daughter offered to relieve me, I felt uncomfortable leaving Mama to be cared for by anyone else. On occasions, I was forced to leave to go to the chiropractor, and every Thursday, my good friend, Betty Arnold, came by to take me out for a few hours. As we got closer to the end, I never left Mama's side.

On Friday, August 1st, Mama hardly moved. I called the nurse that morning and told her that I thought Mama must have slipped into a coma, but when I rolled her on her side to insert a suppository, she said "Ouch!" When the nurse arrived, I laughed as I told her about the incident.

"I guess that means that she's not in a coma," I said.

She listened to Mama's heart, and checked her other vital signs. "She's amazing! As sick as she is, she's got a real strong heart," Connie said.

I sat in the recliner at the foot of her bed, and kept a close eye on the clock to make sure that I didn't skip her medication. Around one-thirty the next morning, she started to make gurgling noises. I thought that she was chocking, and I tried suctioning her mouth out a few times. At six o'clock Saturday morning on August 2nd, I gave her another dose of morphine.

Mama loved cherry and grape Popsicles, and although she was not responsive, I decided to mash some of the sweet ice between my fingers. When I put a little on her tongue, she actually moved her tongue to lick her lips. It made me happy to know that I could give her this tiny pleasure. Art came into the bedroom and took my place in the recliner at the foot of Mama's bed. I was exhausted, so I flopped down on the bed next to Mama's, and fell off to sleep.

I was awakened by a shrill scream as Faith called my name, "Gail!"

I jumped a foot off the bed and stood staring in shock. Faith and Shaun were standing, one on each side of Mama's bed. The room was tight with furniture, and we had pushed Mama's waterbed over, to squeeze in the hospital bed. The two beds were actually touching, so I was lying right beside Mama when she slipped away. They had pulled the hospital bed over so Faith could stand on her right side.

"She's gone," Faith screamed as I ran around to the side of the bed.

"No," I shouted. "How could she die alone? I sat here all night nursing her. I didn't want her to die alone. I promised her that I would be by her side, holding her hand. I was so tired. I just fell off to sleep for a moment." When I looked at the clock, I saw that I'd been asleep for two hours.

I touched Mama's left foot and leg. They were cold. I moved up to caress her face. It was still warm. I then put my ear to her chest, but there was no sound. I stood crying for a while, and my sister and my daughter comforted me.

"You did everything you could," Shaun said.

I took a deep breath and walked over to the telephone. I dialed Art's number. When he answered, a few seconds passed before I could finally form the words. "She's gone," I choked out between sobs.

"We'll be there in a minute," Art said, and the phone went silent.

I pressed the button to get a dial tone, and I phoned the hospice nurse. "Connie, its Gail. Mama's gone," I told her. I gave her a brief account of the events leading up to Mama's death.

"I'm so sorry. I'll notify the coroner and the funeral home, and I'll be there in about twenty minutes," Connie said.

"Thank you," I replied. I hung up the phone, and took my seat in the recliner at the foot of Mama's bed. *It's over,* I thought. There was nothing left for me to do. I thought about the sounds that Mama had made. They must have been the famous death rattle, but I thought that she was choking.

Within a few minutes, Connie walked in. She went around to the side of Mama's bed and listened for life signs. "Yep, she's gone. She was so sweet." Connie bent down and gave Mama a kiss.

I don't think that I could have made it through those last three weeks without her nursing expertise, and her loving heart. She took care of Mama, and she took care of me by comforting me, and assuring me that I could do a good job.

Art and Laverne arrived, and then the coroner came in. Connie and the coroner went through their paperwork, and they checked off and disposed of the remaining narcotics. Shaun combed Mama's hair.

"She wouldn't want anyone to see her in disarray," Shaun said.

The Nurses' Aide came in right in the middle of everything, and she called out to Mama as she normally did. I walked toward the door to stop her, but she had already advanced from the hallway to the entrance of the bedroom. The sight of everyone in the room stopped her sharply, and she let out a gasp.

"Oh no," she moaned.

I grabbed her by the arm, and walked her out to the wheelchair ramp. There I was. I had just lost my mother, but I had time to comfort someone else. I felt sorry for her. She had just lost a husband and a son. She had been so good and gentle to Mama. I knew that this would devastate her, too.

I went back inside and remained in the room until the undertaker arrived. They wrapped Mama in her sheets. They were about to roll in a gurney that was covered with a deep purple, velvet cloth. It was the sight of that cloth that buckled my knees. It consumed me with razor sharp pain that started in the pit of my stomach and rose quickly to my throat. I could not bear to see the gurney. I had to leave the room.

I went to the living room and started telephoning family. I called my Uncle Gene to tell him that his baby sister had gone to glory. I called my other children in New Orleans, Wisconsin, and Florida to tell them that their grandma was no more. My brother and I embraced for a long time.

"Well," I said. "I guess we're the old folks now!"

Art and John had already made funeral arrangements a few weeks before. Mama told us that she wanted to be cremated, and she wanted her ashes thrown into the Pearl River at one of her favorite fishing spots, near the mouth of Lake Bourne. Art asked me if I would go to the funeral home to pick out the urn.

"Do they sell flammable urns?" I asked. "Why would we want an urn anyway, if we're going to dispose of her ashes?"

"I'd like to have it if you don't want it," Art said.

"It's yours," I replied. "I think it would be appropriate for Laverne to come along to help me pick it out, since it will eventually be part of your home decor."

"Absolutely," Art replied. "Just give her a call when you're ready."

Laverne and I went to the funeral home, and we both agreed on an expensive bronze box that displayed a lovely bronze rose.

We set the date for a memorial service, and the following day Art and I worked on the obituary. I typed it up and dropped off a copy at the funeral home and a copy to the printers.

We held the service at Holmes Chapel United Methodist Church on Mama Nettie's birthday, August 8, 2003. It was more like a roast instead of a funeral, and that's exactly what Mama wanted. I composed and typed a little poem on the back of the obituary to eulogize her life.

The following day, a family friend, Jack Lewis, took Art and several of our children out on his boat in the Pearl River. I stayed behind because my back pain had made me too clumsy to board the boat. They sprinkled Mama's ashes there, and Shaun tossed a bunch of long-stemmed red roses into the river.

Everyone was somber and weeping when all of a sudden, the gray ashes seemed to shimmer and take the form of a giant mermaid. The mermaid took off and swam upstream towards the exact spot where Mama and Uncle

Charles had frequently moored his boat when they came out to the river to fish.

Everyone stood gazing in dismay, and suddenly, Shaun burst into laughter. "That's Grandma for you. We should have known that she would let us know if we had put her in the wrong spot." When they returned to the house and told everyone about the mermaid, we all had a good laugh, and everyone knew that Mama would be happy there.

Chapter V

Doing the Right Thing

Comforting the Dying

The year was 1936, and my mother was six years old. One day, Mama Nettie was in the house when she heard a sound outside. She opened the screen door and saw J.C. and Fred peeping through the vertical slats of the wooden gate.

"Miss Nettie," J.C. cried. "Our Mama sent us, and she told us to ask if you will promise to take care of her baby if anything happens to her?"

"Is your Mama sick?" Mama Nettie asked.

"Yes, Miss, she's mighty sick," replied J.C.

"Well, you boys go on home now, and don't worry. You tell your Mama that she's going to be all right." The two small boys turned and ran across the empty field, and down the dusty road to their house.

About 15 minutes later, Mama Nettie heard a tiny voice calling. This time she walked to the gate. J.C. and Fred were standing there again, with tears streaming down their cheeks.

"My goodness!" exclaimed Mama Nettie. "What on earth is wrong with you boys?"

"Our Mama sent us back to ask if you would promise to take care of her baby if anything should happen to her?"

"Now you boys hush that crying. Go home and tell your Mama that nothing is going to happen to her. She will be just fine, and you tell her to stop worrying, I promise to take care of her baby."

Once again, J.C. and Fred turned and ran home. Mama Nettie walked to the side gate and watched them until they were out of sight. She was still standing there, wondering what must be going through Libby's mind, when she caught sight of the two small boys headed back towards the house. Mama Nettie unlatched the gate and stretched it open. J.C. carried a small white bundle in his arms, and Fred had a small package, too. When they reached the gate, J.C. stretched out his arms to give Mama Nettie the tiny baby, and Fred handed her some baby clothes bound in a diaper.

"It's a boy, Miss Nettie, and Mama named him LeNard. Our Mama's dead now."

The two boys wept uncontrollably. My grandmother bent down to hug the crying boys to her, and she knelt there for a long while and prayed for the children who had just lost their mother.

LeNard

We were just little squirts. I couldn't have been much older than three, because my memories are very vague about the goings and comings of a handsome teenager who made kites, and roasted wieners out on the open field for us.

He would dig a big pit in the middle of the field and fill it with logs from the woodpile. After retrieving matches from his pocket, he ignited the wood to get a nice fire going. It was pleasant on those crisp, fall days to feel the warmth of the fire against my hands and cheeks. Then LeNard would produce a few wieners, and spear them on sticks that he had whittled to make a sharp point.

"Okay! Now just hold the wieners over the fire and turn the stick slowly to let them cook," LeNard instructed.

I was so excited to be cooking my own meal, and my mouth watered as the juice bubbled out of the meat and made a searing sound as it hit the hot embers.

By the time I turned five, he disappeared from our household. I was too young to even notice his absence, but when I was older I learned that he had joined the Marine Corps.

LeNard was just a few years old when my mother sat him on the piano stool next to her, and taught him to play the Boogie Woogie. Music would later become an integral part of his life, and when he returned from Korea, he played gigs in the French Quarter of New Orleans and area bars. Later, he taught himself to play the bass guitar, and started his own Blues band that he called Bo Peters' & Friends.

LeNard traveled around the world with his band, playing in Japan, England, and as far away as Australia. He slowed down after having a stroke in 1998, but he continues to play, and he can never resist the urge to perform whenever he's around music.

Feeding the Hungry

We were happy in our little world when we lived with my grandparents. Our daily routines were like most toddlers. We were up as soon as the sun rose, and after a hearty breakfast of oatmeal, or grits with milk and sugar, or bacon and eggs, we trailed Dad out to the chicken yard.

Mama Nettie cleaned the kitchen, and put on a pot of beans so they would be done by lunchtime. The only variation in the noontime meal was in the variety of beans. Every day, except Sunday, we ate a hot bowl of beans and rice with cornbread, or buttered slices of white bread. Monday was always red bean day, but the rest of the week, we ate butter beans, pinto beans, black-eyed peas, great northern white beans or little, brown beans called crowder peas.

Dad cut roots from the tall, thin sassafras trees that grew in the woods. He used a sharp ax to cut thick chips from the pale wood, and when Mama Nettie boiled the fragrant chips or a chunk of the bark to make tea, the pale wood turned a pinkish-orange color. They also mixed the extract of sassafras roots with water, sugar, and yeast to make root beer. A few chunks of ice were chipped from the big block that sat in the icebox, and we drank cool root beer or fresh lemonade with our noonday meals. Everyone took a nap after lunch, and when we woke up, we were anxious to get outside for a couple of hours of playtime.

Supper was always a treat. Mama Nettie prepared turnip greens, field peas that grew in long, green pods or some other fresh vegetable like yellow squash, corn cooked with fresh tomatoes and onions, or fresh snap beans with new potatoes. My favorite meat was pork chops. There was always rice and gravy or a baked sweet potato. Sometimes, she would slice the sweet potatoes and fry them too, or we would have a fried banana-like fruit called a plantain as a side dish. We drank hot sassafras tea with our evening meals, and there was always a pie or some bread pudding for dessert.

One evening, Mama Nettie had supper going. She sat the round tub in the middle of the kitchen floor to give us a bath before we ate, and Art and I giggled as she scrubbed our feet.

"You're as shinny as two new pennies," she said, as she dried us off and dressed us. "Now you go to the living room to play until I call you for supper."

Off we ran, still giggling, and admiring the new pajamas that our mother had made for us.

We heard the dogs sounding the alarm outside, and Dad went to investigate. He came inside, and crossed through the living room to the kitchen. Within a few seconds, Mama Nettie and Dad went outside and walked to the front gate. A tall, thin man stood on the opposite side of the gate, and we peeked around the doorsill to see what was going on. We could see an old truck, but we could not make out who was inside.

"Good evening sir," Mama Nettie said. "My husband tells me that you and your family are in need of some food, and a place to stay for the night."

"Yes, Missus, we've been traveling all day, and the wife and children are mighty tired and hungry. I'm headed to my folks in Hattiesburg to get work, and we're plum out of money. I sure would appreciate it if you folks could give us a hand."

We never knew if the strangers saw a star shining over the old house, or if they had stopped to ask someone else who told them where they could certainly find help. One thing for sure, they had come to the right spot.

"Come on in, and make yourselves at home." Mama Nettie said. "Supper is just about ready."

The stranger, his wife, and three small children about our size followed us inside, and the mother held an infant in her arms. A ceramic basin sat on a small stand in the front bedroom. Dad filled the basin with water, and laid a few linen towels on the bed for the strangers to freshen up.

Mama Nettie returned to the kitchen and performed some miracle to increase the supper that was originally prepared for four to a meal for nine. When everything was ready, we all took our places around the long wooden table, and my grandmother began dishing up plates for everyone. Dad said the blessing, and asked for the Lord's help and protection for the strangers as they traveled over the highways.

Through the dim light of the oil lanterns, I caught sight of the mother sitting directly in front of me. She opened her blouse, and put the baby to her chest. I was stunned, and I dropped my fork to stare at this strange act. This was the first time that I had seen a baby nurse and absolutely the first time that I had ever seen a naked human breast, too.

"Mind your manners, and stop that staring," Mama Nettie said to me with a stern voice.

I picked up my fork and began to eat again, but I could not resist the urge to peek when I thought no one was looking.

I remember well that Art had taken his milk from a bottle because I would stick my hand through the slats of our cribs, and steal that bottle as often as I could. I'd rush to take a couple of good slurps of the warm, sweet fluid before he let out a yelp to bring my grandmother running into the room. I had already thrown the bottle back into Art's crib before Mama Nettie could get to me.

"Did you take that baby's bottle again, gal?" she would ask.

I would lie there looking as innocent as a newborn lamb, and she would put the bottle back into Art's mouth and leave the room.

After supper, Mama Nettie pulled out quilts and pillows, and the mother put her children down for the night.

We said our prayers, "And God bless our mama, our daddy, Mama Nettie and Dad, and everybody in the whole wide world." Before long, I was dreaming about the Tin Man on stilts as he appeared on the cover of my favorite book, *The Wizard of Oz.*

The next morning, we were back at the table for breakfast, and Mama Nettie packed some food for the strangers to take with them. We never saw them again, but I often wonder if they had been lucky enough to find another family as generous as my dear grandparents.

Calming My Fears

Our little lives were filled with sunshine, blooming flowers, happy sounds, and smells of the old house and Mama Nettie's cooking. The biggest treat for us every year was attending the Annual Gulfside Picnic in Waveland, Mississippi. The picnic was sponsored by my grandparents' church. It was great, but the most exciting part for me was getting to swim in the murky waters of the Gulf.

The waters of the Gulf are not clean, but they are translucent enough that you can still see your feet to a depth of about a foot or two. Though my grandfather kept a close watch on us to make certain that we did not wander too far, it was necessary to walk out at least 100 feet from shore before we could reach waist-deep water. I loved to swim.

"Look, Dad! I'm swimming," I screamed to my grandfather as he sat on the steps of the seawall.

Dad would wave back at me with a big grin and yell, "Yes! You're swimming like a fish."

My grandmother walked across the road to call us when it was time to eat.

"Can I stay in a while longer?" I asked.

"It's time to eat now. You can get back in the water later on."

Obediently, I climbed up the seawall, and my grandmother wrapped a warm towel around my shoulders.

Mama Nettie went over to the wooden ice cream maker, and gently raised the steel container above the soupy mixture of ice, and rock salt. She unscrewed the frothy lid, and pulled out the dasher. It was covered with thick cream and bright, yellow chunks of fresh peaches.

"Can I lick the dasher, Mama Nettie?" I squealed with glee. Art and I dove in, and we licked and wiped the frozen dasher until it was as clean as a new whistle.

I was itchy about getting back to swimming, but Mama Nettie made us wait two hours after eating.

"Is it time yet?" I'd ask every ten minutes until we were finally allowed to return to the water.

The Pearl River was only a few blocks away from the old house, but we were not allowed to swim in the river. We went to the river to fish, but we never had any desire to swim in those muddy, snake and gator-infested waters.

"Stay away from the river. It's too deep, and it has whirlpools and a swift current," Mama Nettie told us.

There were teenagers in the neighborhood that did swim in the river, and one summer night, one of the neighborhood boys drowned. The men of Pearlington pulled their drag nets through the water for seven days before they found his body. On the night that they found him,

I overheard my grandparents talking as they always did when they retired for the evening.

"He was a pitiful sight," Dad said. "His poor body was swollen beyond recognition, and the crabs had eaten away his ears and fingers."

I was traumatized about Bobby's death. He had been a handsome boy, and now it was painful, and frightening, for me to imagine what had happened to him. After that night, I could no longer get into the water. Whenever we went to the beach, I refused to go for a swim, and on one occasion when Dad forced me to get into the water, I screamed and cried, "The crabs are going to eat me. I don't want to swim anymore."

It took me 45 years to overcome my fear of the water, and I started swimming again just after my 50th birthday. I consider this to be my most successful feat, and every time I enter the water, I can still hear my grandfather's shout, "You're swimming like a fish."

I've already stated over and over that I was always afraid of something. When Art and I had our cribs safely tucked in the corner of my grandparent's bedroom, with the exception of the shadows, I felt relatively secure. Once we were moved out to the living room, I was always petrified. The great source of my fear was "the voice."

Every night I was awakened by the sound of barking dogs, and then I would hear the bellowing voice of a man speaking to me. I would cover my ears and cry hysterically while the voice rambled on. I would roll myself up tightly in the covers, from head to toe, and pray that the voice could not see me.

One hot summer night, Mama Nettie passed through the room and saw me completely enveloped in the sheet. "Come out!" she said, "You're going to smother in there."

"I'm scared. The voice is going to get me."

"What voice? There's no one here except your brother, Dad and me. Now you unwrap yourself right this minute." Reluctantly, I emerged from my protective cocoon, and Mama Nettie removed the top sheet from my bed. "It's too hot for all of this, now you get back to sleep. It's late."

I tried to fall asleep, but I was overcome with fear. Eventually, I slid between the bottom sheet and the plastic cover of the couch, and I was finally able to fall off to sleep. The following night, I returned to the same position and was sweating profusely long before the voice returned to haunt me. Once again, Mama Nettie passed through and caught me.

"My goodness, what on earth are you doing now? Give me that sheet."

The fear closed tightly around me I could feel the darkness of the room on my bare flesh and I lay rigid and petrified. I guess I dozed off, but the menacing voice returned. I cried and tossed on the couch, but there was nothing that I could do. Art lay sleeping across the room on another couch, but I was frozen, and I knew that he was too small to save me anyway.

The voice continued to bellow out wordless sounds, and finally, I mustered up enough courage to seek refuge. Mama Nettie had picked out the brown and tan plastic to hide the worn red cover of the old couch. The heavy plastic cover was simply draped over the back and the bottom of the couch, and fixed with brass, upholstery tacks.

The couch opened down by pulling the back slightly forward to unlock the mechanism, and the entire back laid down flat to form the bed like our modern day futons. The plastic was not fixed on the ends at the site of the wooden arms of the couch, so I managed to wiggle my thin body underneath the slack of the plastic at that opening. I slid down like a little worm until I was securely hidden head to toe.

Mama Nettie was always up early to start breakfast, and she found me buried under the plastic cover the following morning.

"My Lord, what have I done," she cried. She pulled me out and rocked me in her arms. "Don't worry, you can have your cover back tonight," she said.

I lay there in the security and comfort of her arms, and was happy that I would have my protective shield back once again.

Chapter VI

Sheltering the Homeless

Rescuing an Old Man

In 1912, Mama Adelaide met and married a man from Gulfport named Ezekiel Evans. They had a son the following year in 1913, whom they named Ezekiel Evans, Jr., and they lived together as servants for a wealthy Pearlington gentleman by the name of Coburn Weston.

Pappy Zeek, as everyone called him, was a carpenter, and he taught his young son the trade. Pappy was tall, and extremely thin. He had the high cheekbones and nose of most of the folks in the area. His skin was dark with a tinge of red, and he was bald on top with a ring of straight hair that hung down on the nape of his neck.

Like many of the Indians, Pappy drank his share of corn whiskey, but he was a gentle, quiet spirit, and was probably a little too passive for my great-grandmother's liking.

Mama Nettie told me that Pappy would sit on the front porch, smoking his pipe, while Mama Adelaide sat in the parlor in her rocking chair. She would be screaming loud enough to be heard a mile down the road.

"Help, save me. He's killing me. Help me, Lord save me."

Mama Nettie would walk over to their house, and whisper to Pappy, "What's wrong with Mama now?"

Pappy pointed his chin in the direction of the living room and shook his head. "Only the good Lord knows!"

Anyone passing on the road just smiled Pappy's way, and continued on their journey. No one dared to stop. Not even the sheriff was brave enough to pass by when "Miss Liete," as many people called her, was on one of her rampages.

The marriage didn't last, and eventually Pappy Zeek left Pearlington. He was gone for more than 30 years when Mama Nettie received word from a neighbor that they had seen Pappy in his hometown of Gulfport, Mississippi. "He looks real sick, and he can't walk. Folks say that he's homeless, too."

When my grandparents heard this, they knew that there was only one thing to do. They would go to Gulfport to find Pappy and bring him home to live with them.

One fall day in 1951, Mama Nettie called Art and me into the living room. She was sitting in her armless rocking chair, and she held her arms out to us. We stood beside her as she hugged us tightly, and she told us about her stepfather's misfortune.

"Now I've always told you children about God and His goodness. He has blessed all of us with good health, a home, food, and clothes. He gives us all that we need, but sometimes there are people who are not as fortunate as we are, and it is up to us to help them. I have a stepfather who's sick, and he does not have a home, so Dad and I have decided to bring him to live with us. We will all get up real early tomorrow morning and take a trip to find Pappy."

We were excited about the long trip, even though Gulfport was only 40 miles away to the east. Everyone was up early, and Mama Nettie called us for breakfast. She gave us bowls of grits with strips of bacon, and thick biscuits dripping with homemade butter. There was a jar of fig preserves, and lots of the sweet, dark molasses made from our last sugarcane crop sat on the table, too. Dad had a steaming cup of coffee. He liked it when the cream boiled to the top of the milk, and formed a thin, tan skin that floated in the top of his coffee cup. Art and I ate hurriedly because we were anxious to get started.

Mama Nettie packed a basket with sliced liver cheese and pressed ham, bread, pound cake and grapes. She used an ice pick to chop a few chunks from the big block of ice, and she poured lemonade and ice into a tall, silver thermos.

Dad walked out to his old Dodge, paneled truck. He flung open the two back doors and removed one of the wooden benches that lined the side walls. He entered the house again, and came out a few minutes later carrying a mattress.

"Why are we taking a bed?" I asked.

"Pappy is sick, and he may need to lay down when we find him," Dad replied.

Art and I perched ourselves on the other bench, and Dad closed the back doors of the truck. Mama Nettie took her place on the front seat and she turned to put the basket on the floor beside us. Everything was ready, and off we went. The beautiful, scenic drive along the white sand beaches of the Gulf Coast seemed like a very long journey to Art and me.

Searching for Pappy

Gulfport was an enormous city, compared to the tall yellow pine trees of little Pearlington. The big buildings, which couldn't have stood more than six floors, seemed like skyscrapers to us. We made several stops, and Dad got out each time. We could hear the muffled conversations as he asked strangers for information concerning Pappy's whereabouts. We searched all morning, and they were just about to give up when Mama Nettie said, "Let's make one more stop." We saw two ladies sitting on their front porch, and Mama Nettie pointed in their direction. "There," she cried. "Go ask those ladies!"

Dad pulled the truck to the side of the road, and headed across the street. He stopped at the gate and greeted the women.

"Good day!" he said. "We are searching for my wife's step-daddy, and we were told that he is staying in this area in an abandoned house, but we have not been able to find him. Could you ladies be of help?" he asked. They continued to talk, and finally Dad turned to come back to the truck, but this time he had a big grin on his face.

Dad jumped in behind the wheel and started the truck. "Well, I've got good news. Those ladies told me that we are very close to the old house," Dad said. "We must look for an old broken mail box on the left side of the road. It should be just ahead."

Off we went to get Pappy. We traveled a short distance and stopped again. Tall bamboo canes grew along both sides of the road, and although we had driven past this area several times, no house was visible from the road.

"Let's go!" Dad said, and we all climbed out of the truck. There was a tiny footpath through the bamboo and thick weeds. *Is this the jungle?* I thought. Dad led the way. Soon we reached an unpainted shell of a house, and we stepped into an empty room. Even at our young ages, Art was three and I was four, we knew that the shack that we had just entered was a miserable excuse for a shelter. There were no windows or doors, and for the most part, there was no floor or roof either. Thick, green vines grew through the openings and crept throughout the house. The place stank of urine and human excrement, combined with the odor of decaying wood and mildew.

We stepped into the second room and there he was, lying on a pile of rags.

"Pappy," Mama Nettie called. "It's Daughter, and we've come to take you home."

He rose up on his left elbow from his wretched bed and mumbled something to them.

He was thin with his half-ring of long white hair and a short, scraggly white beard. Pappy pointed to a big white cloth bundled up in a corner of the room. Dad put the bundle under his arm, and slowly, with Dad on one side, and Mama Nettie on the other, they helped Pappy Zeek out to the truck. Dad opened the back doors, and Pappy crawled in on the mattress. Art and I fixed ourselves on the bench and stared at the strange, unkempt man who smelled like soiled baby diapers, and who could not use his legs.

We drove west down the coast for a while and passed through Long Beach and Pass Christian. We crossed the long drawbridge to Bay St. Louis, and took a left turn down the beach road until we reached Waveland. Dad pulled over and stopped the truck under a big oak tree at Gulfside.

Gulfside was a section along the beach that belonged to the Black Methodist Assembly. This part of the beach was always reserved for black folks. Later, the spot would be a part of Buccaneer State Park, and after Katrina, there would be nothing left.

Mama Nettie spread an old blanket on the grass, and she pulled out the basket while Pappy sat at the back of the truck, dangling his limp limbs. We sipped the cool lemonade and ate sandwiches, fruit, and a slice of buttery pound cake. When we were done, Dad pulled out his Bible to read, while Mama Nettie and Pappy chatted, and Art and I ran around chasing dragonflies. After our little picnic, we headed out to make the 16-mile trip home.

Over the next year or so, Dad placed the mattress in the back of the old truck, and he and Mama Nettie went off to make frequent visits to the doctor with Pappy. Pappy Zeek hobbled around on his crutches and spent most of his time resting. He sent us to the store to buy the little, white sacks of "Bull Durum" tobacco, and we would watch in amazement as he rolled the dark, sweet-smelling tobacco in the thin strips of paper, and gave the paper a final lick to make it stick.

We didn't know it then, but Pappy was only one of a long stream of strangers who were destined to enter our home and our hearts. My grandparents cared for him for the next six years until his death in 1957.

I was 10 years old when he died, and that Friday night I went to Pappy's wake with Mama and my stepfather, Ben. When we got to Mama Nettie's house, I was amazed to see the transformation. All of the furniture had been removed from my grandparent's bedroom. The door between the entrance hallway and the bedroom had been removed and placed atop three wooden carpenter's sawhorses. Sheets were draped over the door, and the coffin was placed on top.

Pappy was laid out in a dark suit, and a nice tie was knotted around his thin neck His rim of white hair was slicked back, and the top of his head formed a shiny sphere under the glow of the single light bulb. Neighbors, and lots of strangers, entered the house and filed one-by-one past the gray coffin. I stood across the room and stared at the corpse, and I wondered if anyone had remembered to dress Pappy in his suspenders and socks.

The following day, we returned to Pearlington for the funeral. There was a fence around the family plot, but the cemetery caretakers had dug a deep hole outside the fence for Pappy. Pearlington sits about thirteen feet below sea level, and at least three feet of water stood in the hole. When the undertakers lowered the casket into the grave, it made a big splash and bounced back up near the top of the grave.

I'll never forget that sight. That day, my grandmother declared that she didn't want to be buried in the ground. That day, I figured that I'd better learn how to swim again real soon. I decided that wakes and funerals were uncivilized practices, so I made a vow to myself that I would not attend another one if I could help it.

A few years later, while walking through the cemetery with Mama Nettie, I asked her if Pappy had been buried outside the fence of the family plot because Mama

Adelaide feared that all of her husbands would be fighting over her.

My grandmother laughed that sweet, joyous tune, and told me that there would be no fighting in heaven. "All earthly things will pass away, and only the glory of the Lord will be manifested."

By then, Papa Phillip, Pappy Zeek and Mr. Arthur Acker, her third husband, were all buried in the same area at Pearlington Cemetery. There would be one more husband to bury, but Mama Adelaide would not be around for that funeral. In 1960, she married Mr. Oscar White. He would have been the only one to see the goose pick the grass from Mama Adelaide's grave, except for the fact that he was as blind as a bat.

Ernie

Ernestine Spears lived with her mother in Bay St. Louis. Her father died a year or so before, and her mother was ill and could not take care of her. Therefore, my grandparents did what they had always done. They opened their hearts and their home to someone less fortunate.

Pappy was with us about six months when Mama Nettie and Dad took Ernie in. Ernie was born on December 1, 1945, so we were only thirteen months apart. She was tall and lanky, and wore her shoulder-length hair turned under in a "pageboy." Art and I were thrilled to have another companion, and for us, Ernie would always be our sister. The year was 1952, and that was the birth of "The Three Pioneers," which is what we chose to call ourselves.

Ernie fit right in. She taught me how to roll my hair on twisted pieces of brown paper sacks. We did everything together. Mama Nettie taught us both how to make biscuits, and soon that became our daily chore. She was the older sister that Art and I never had. It was as though she had always been a part of our lives, and it's hard to remember life before her. Even though I left Pearlington a few years later, we saw each other often and stayed close.

Years later, Ernie's mother would move to Pearlington, and Mama Nettie and Dad took her in and helped her to get on her feet. Ernie remained with my grandparents until she graduated from Valena C. Jones High School and attended business school in Gulfport, Mississippi. She married her childhood sweetheart, Willie (Billy) Peters. Billy was the son of the sugarcane mill owner, Mr. Percy Peters. They built a house in Pearlington where they raised their four children: Willie, Jr., Ladonna, Angela and Elaine.

Ernie did have a biological brother named Hilton Spears. I don't know the circumstances of their separation, but she searched for him for many years. She moved to Chicago, Illinois because she traced him there. Unfortunately, a house fire destroyed everything they had in Chicago, and Art picked them up and took Ernie and her family to Jackson, Michigan.

Ernie worked as a seamstress in a sewing factory, and in retail for many years. She was always a joyful person who brought light into every room. Ernie's short life came to an end on September 5, 2001 when she lost a battle with cancer. Ironically, her brother, Hilton, who had searched for her for more than 40 years, called one of her daughters a day or two before her funeral. At last he had found her, but now it was too late. Evidently he had moved from Chicago to California shortly before Ernie had gone up north to search for him, and sadly, their paths never crossed.

If Hilton should read this book one day, I want him to know that his sister loved him and never ceased to think of him. I hope that this message will give him some closure and peace of mind. I hope, too, that he will be pleased to know that Ernie grew up in a loving family. Though Ernie was officially our aunt, before she died she helped her children with her obituary. She wanted Art and me to be listed as her brother and sister, and it made me happy to know that death has no power over love.

Kenny

Ernie had been with us for a few months when we were all gathered around the supper table for an announcement.

"Well, I've got some news for you children," said Mama Nettie. "We received word from the Welfare Department that there is a baby boy who has no mother or father, so Dad and I want to give him a home."

We listened carefully as Mama Nettie explained that Kenny was one of God's special children. He had some birth defects that had injured his brain, and he was unable to perform as a normal baby his age. The welfare workers told her that the baby would never be able to walk, talk, or function normally.

"We must all try to help Kenny, because he has no one else to love or care for him," grandmother said.

We all felt extremely sorry for the new baby, and on the day that the welfare lady pulled up, Ernie, Art and I were lined up at the gate to get a first glimpse of the little boy with the damaged brain. Kenny had a big head covered with reddish blond curls that were so tight, we called them "B.B. shots." His thin, white body was completely out of proportion to his oversized head, and his enormous green eyes stared back at us. He looked kind of funny, but we were relieved to see that his brains were not hanging out.

We lived up to Mama Nettie's expectations, and helped her with Kenny as much as we could. One day, Ernie and I decided to try our hand at changing his diaper. We laid him on Mama Nettie's bed, and Ernie removed the soiled diaper. We lifted him up and placed the clean diaper under him, and pulled at the cloth to make the ends overlap. Ernie got the safety pin in the left side without a hitch, but when she moved to the right side, Kenny let out a scream that filled us all with terror. Art was standing nearby, and we were all trying to figure out what could be wrong with the freshly diapered baby. We picked him up and walked around the room, but he continued to squall. Finally, we decided to lay him down and check the pins. Sure enough, poor Kenny was pinned to his diaper. There was no blood, and he stopped crying as soon as Ernie removed the pin. From that day on, we decided to limit our help to holding his bottle and pushing him about in the stroller.

Kenny thrived under Mama Nettie's care, but soon the Welfare Department picked him up and took him all the way out to California to be checked by a specialist there. The doctors reconfirmed the original diagnosis. Kenny was severely brain damaged at birth, and there was no hope for him.

Despite the medical prognostications, Mama Nettie worked hard with Kenny, and by the time he was two years old he could walk. His speech was difficult because he stuttered, but we managed to understand his limited vocabulary. The doctors told Mama Nettie that his vision was poor too, and he was fitted for thick glasses that were held to his head by a piece of elastic. Within another year, Kenny was potty trained and things got a little easier for all of us.

One day, Mama Nettie received a call from the Welfare Department. They were coming for Kenny to place him in another foster home. Mama Nettie and Dad were heartbroken, and there was a gloom in the house for weeks after his departure.

"I don't understand it. Why would they take him away from us when he's doing so well?" Mama Nettie wondered out loud.

Nearly two years had passed when my grandmother received a call from the Welfare folks. They informed her that Kenny had completely reverted to his infantile state. He was no longer potty trained, and he would not walk or speak. His new foster parent could not handle him.

"Will you take him back?" asked the Welfare worker.

Mama Nettie told her that she would have to discuss the matter with Dad, and call her back. That night they made their decision, and the following morning Mama Nettie gave her reply.

"We will take Kenny back under one condition only. You must allow us to adopt him because we never want him to be snatched from us again."

There was a law on the books in Mississippi, which stated that mentally retarded children could not be adopted. The welfare people made a lot of promises that day, and it took nearly a year before the paperwork went through, but at last, he was officially Kenny Giles.

Shortly after Kenny came home, Mama Nettie told Dad that she missed having a dining room because they had sacrificed the old dining room to create a bedroom for Pappy. Dad always did what he could to make my grandmother happy, so he figured out a plan to rearrange the walls in the old house to accommodate a new dining room.

Workers came from Picayune, Mississippi with big jacks. They raised the house, and put new pilings and sills in strategic places to allow them to redistribute the center point of the foundation. The wall that separated the hallway from Mama Nettie and Dad's bedroom was pushed over to create two rooms equal in size. A new entrance doorway was cut from the window that overlooked the front porch in my grandparent's bedroom. Their bedroom was now transformed into the living room, and the enlarged entranceway was now their bedroom. The old living room became the dining room.

By 1959, Kenny was nearly seven years old, and he had developed normal motor skills. Though his speech impediment was still a problem, it had improved greatly, and his vocabulary had expanded. Kenny could run, laugh and play with the other children now. He was able to start school the following year.

Our favorite time of the year had rolled around again, and the long pastry table was laid out in the new dining room. One afternoon during the Christmas holiday season, Ernie, Art and I helped Mama Nettie clear away the dinner dishes and we were all sitting in the living room. As usual, Dad sat with his Bible in his lap and nodded as he pretended to read. Mama Nettie sat in her rocking chair crocheting wool caps for us, while we sat on the floor playing jacks, pick-up-sticks and building houses with our log cabin erector set. We looked at Mama Nettie and laughed with her whenever Dad let out a little snort, and his head bobbed up and down like a duck drinking water.

No one noticed when Kenny disappeared from the room, but when Mama Nettie looked up from her crocheting, she asked, "Now where is that boy?"

We all looked up and then went back to our games. Mama Nettie set her crocheting on the table next to her and got up to look for Kenny. When she walked into the dining room, there he was, standing at the pastry table, shoveling a handful of chocolate cake into his mouth.

"What in the world are you doing?" asked Mama Nettie. Kenny jumped back from the table, and Mama Nettie saw that he had eaten about one-fourth of the formerly untouched cake.

"I'm going to teach you a lesson," said Mama Nettie. "You must never touch things without asking permission. Now you sit right down to this table. You're going to eat this whole cake." She sliced the cake into chunks and handed Kenny a spoon.

"Now you get to eating Mister," Mama Nettie ordered. She stood at the opposite end of the table with her arms crossed and watched as Kenny devoured every crumb of the chocolate cake.

When he was done, he licked his lips and rolled those enormous green eyes up to Mama Nettie, and said, "Ma-a-a-ma Nettie, can I have a piece of pie?"

"Well," Mama Nettie concluded, "I've never been so outdone in all my days!"

We laughed for hours that evening as Mama Nettie recounted the incident to us. Not only was Kenny smart, he was smarter than any of us, because he was definitely the first of us children to pull the wool over Mama Nettie's eyes. He knew how to get his cake and eat it too.

Kenny is still considered mentally handicapped, but his disability is barely noticeable. He graduated from high school, holds down a job, and is able to manage his life with some supervision. Mama Nettie proved that even impossible odds could be conquered with prayer, persistence and love.

Chapter VII

Familiar Surroundings

The Old House

There were no street signs back then, but Mama Nettie and Dad's old house was located in Pearlington on Hancock Street. After passing the main section of town where the stores were located, you had to make a right turn on Whites Road. Hancock Street runs parallel to Highway 604, and it is the first block down Whites Road. From Whites Road, you take a left turn on Hancock Street. The Odd Fellows Hall was located on the first lot, and my grandparent's house sat on the second lot from the corner.

Mama Nettie and Dad's house seemed enormous to me back then. Before Dad made structural changes, there was a long entranceway with a massive wooden door. The top portion of the door held garnet and amber colored glass. I would lie on the cool linoleum floor and stare at the glass for hours as the afternoon sun filtered through the colored panes, creating mystical patterns on the hallway walls.

A chaise lounge sat under a window that overlooked the side yard, and Mama Nettie's Singer Sewing Machine sat on the opposite wall. Art and I would sit under the sewing machine and rock back and forth on the big pedal. It was there that my grandmother made clothes for us.

You had to make a left turn to enter the next room. This was my grandparent's bedroom. The room was large, and the furniture seemed to be as big as dinosaurs. A four-poster bed and a big chest of drawers occupied the rest of the space in the bedroom, and oh yes, I almost forgot, my grandmother's cedar chest. It sat at the foot of the bed, and that was where she kept all of her important documents, personal treasures, coin and stamp collections and photographs of the entire family.

When Art and I were smaller, we had side-by-side cribs in one corner of the room. My bed was close to the window, and I was always frightened because on moonlit nights the shadows from the window filled the room with grotesque monsters. There was a large fireplace in the room, too, though I never recall seeing a fire lit there.

A strange, black table sat next to the bed. Wooden eagles were carved at the base of each table leg, and each eagle grasped a large glass ball in its claws. The top of the table was covered with a white linen cloth. After the installation of electricity, a big radio held its place of prestige on the tabletop. I can still hear the whining and buzzing of the old radio as Dad turned the dial to find his favorite station every night.

We kids didn't care much for the nightly news, but Sunday evenings were always a thrill as we sat on the floor beside the bed to hear The Jack Benny Show, and Amos and Andy. It was hard for me to understand the punch lines, and I'm still trying to figure out why Rochester was stuck on Jack Benny's roof.

The next room in the house was the living room. It sat directly behind the bedroom, and the fireplace was back-to-back with the one on the other side of the wall in my grandparent's bedroom. A framed tapestry hung over the fireplace. The tapestry depicted an English countryside scene with tall trees, flowers, a stream and a stone footbridge.

The large room was the same width as my grandparent's bedroom. It housed two large sofas, miscellaneous chairs and tables, and Mama Nettie's armless rocker. My grandmother treasured a small wooden coffee table with a glass top, and it sat on display near one of the couches.

That coffee table would cause us a lot of grief within a couple of years.

One of our Saturday morning chores was to oil the furniture in this room, and we would drown every inch of wood in Red Cedar Furniture Polish. When Art and I were finally booted from the cribs, we slept in this great room on the couches, which opened up to form beds by night.

The kitchen was a big room behind the living room, and it was once the dining room. There was nothing particular about it, but I do remember the long, wooden table where we shared our meals. The one thing that really impressed me about the kitchen was the way the dishtowels hung frozen on winter mornings. It was really cold in the old house when the fires were doused for the evening. Fortunately, we had enough comforters and quilts to keep us toasty warm and safe during those long, winter nights.

Mama Nettie sewed brightly colored quilt patches together on her sewing machine, and she would stuff wool between the patchwork and the backing of the quilt. Those quilts were so heavy that it was almost impossible to turn over once we were tucked into bed. To this day, I cannot go to sleep unless I can cover up with a quilt that's heavy enough to make me feel the way I did at Mama Nettie's house.

Another room stood off the kitchen to the right. It was originally the kitchen, but when Pappy Zeek came to live with us, it was converted to his bedroom, and the kitchen was moved to the dining room. There was a screened porch behind the current kitchen, which ran across the back of the house. Eventually, they would divide the porch and glass in a section to make a bedroom for Art. Basically, the house was shaped in the form of a "u."

There was a large, front porch, and the roof formed a high pitch for the attic. Carved eaves and gables ran along the roofline and across the front porch. The house was painted white with dark green trim. The roof of the house was made of tin, and when it rained or hailed, the elements played echoing tunes throughout the old house.

We used an outhouse for toilet duties, and we bathed in a big, tin tub in the kitchen. When I was six years old, Dad and my Uncle Gene added a bathroom onto the house just behind the main entrance hall. It had cold running water only. During the winter months, Mama Nettie heated big kettles of water on the stove, but when it was hot outside, we just filled the tub with cold water, and smuggled a cup of Tide Detergent to the bathroom to take a luxurious bubble bath.

A wire fence enclosed the front yard, and there was a brick walkway leading up to the steps. Privet hedges lined the walkway, and off to the left stood a massive cedar tree. We built a wooden platform across two sturdy limbs of the cedar. The platform was our secret spying station. We often sat quietly and watched everything around us, or we would climb to her wispy top to sway in the afternoon breeze.

There was a large side yard filled with flowers and a pecan tree. We always picked enough pecans from that tree to pay the taxes on the house every year. Just outside the fence to the right of the house stood a 200-year-old oak tree, with great clumps of gray Spanish moss on it. A large, wooden building sat on the lot behind the oak tree. The windows had wooden shutters and there was a massive double door at the entrance. The building belonged to the Masonic Order, The Grand United Order of Odd Fellows.

A tall, wire fence ran across the narrow back yard that separated the chicken yard from the house. A shed stood to the left of the entrance of the yard, and there was a big chicken house next to the shed. There was another fence that ran through the middle of the chicken yard to separate the chickens from the ducks and geese, and there was a big covered area to the right where Dad parked the old truck. We had to walk straight through the chicken yard to reach the garden fields. There, Dad planted sugar cane, corn, tomatoes, Irish potatoes, sweet potatoes, beans, squash, watermelons and greens. We kids did a lot of farming on those few acres, but back then, it seemed more like a hundred.

Mama Nettie told me that when she received the deed to the property she had the land surveyed, and to her great surprise, the deed included the house plus three additional parcels of land for a total of four acres. Dad and my uncles dug holes to place large posts, and they stretched a wire fence around the entire property.

About a year later, the former owner was passing through Pearlington and stopped by for a visit. He stood, leaning on the front gate, as he talked to my grandmother. Finally, his curiosity got the best of him.

"Tell me, what's all this land you got fenced in here?" he asked.

"Why it's the land that you sold to me," Mama Nettie replied.

The gentleman was apparently stunned, but he said nothing more on the subject. It took him several minutes to clear his throat, and finally, he mustered up a faint smile, tipped his hat and turned to walk down the road.

Chapter VIII

Adventures and Mishaps

The Tent

Pappy Zeek was crippled and used crutches to get around. He managed to walk about the house with the use of a cane, but he always used his crutches whenever he went outside.

Pappy still had that beautiful, white canvas that his clothes were bundled in on the day that we brought him home to live with us. When he lived in the old, abandoned house, he used it to protect himself from the rain. Now, he used it to make a pallet, and he would spread it on the ground outside the front yard under the great oak tree. Every day at exactly three o'clock, he would lay his crutches down beside him and take his afternoon nap, or he would just sit on the canvas and watch the people as they passed by on Whites Road.

We were always excited to see the great canvas, and every day we would worry Pappy to let us borrow it.

"Pappy," asked Art, "can we use your canvas to make a tent?"

"Ah! It would make a fine tent indeed, but I'll never give my canvas over to you brats. Now scat before I hit you with my crutch."

One day, Mama Nettie and Dad called us.

"We're taking Pappy to the doctor. Now, you children stay here in the front yard to play. We'll be back in about an hour."

We stood at the gate and watched patiently as they helped Pappy climb into the back of the old Dodge truck. Off they drove down the dusty road. They turned the corner, and we looked at each other and broke into wide grins.

"Let's get the canvas!"

We ran off to Pappy's room, and there it was, neatly folded on a chair near the window. "This will make a great tent," I said. "Let's take it out to the chicken yard. We'll have lots of room there. We can play for a little while, and then we'll just get the canvas back to Pappy's room before they get back. He won't even know that we borrowed it."

Ernie grabbed the canvas, and we all ran out to the chicken yard. We tied the back of the canvas to the wire fence that separated the chicken and duck yards. Everyone went out to scout for poles, and within a few minutes, we had erected the biggest, most beautiful tent ever.

We ran out again to look for objects to make furniture. Art brought boards and cinder blocks, and we made benches and a table. We decided that we needed a stove, too, so Ernie and I dug a deep pit. Art ran to the woodpile, while we stuffed the pit with old newspapers and twigs.

"Let's make a fire!" I exclaimed, and I ran to retrieve matches from the kitchen.

The tent was ready, but we still needed a car, so we cut a limb from a small tree and nailed an old pie pan on top to make a steering wheel. We stuck sticks in the ground to imitate the gas, brake and clutch pedals. Everything was now ready for the pretend games to begin.

Art jumped in his car to drive off to work, and Ernie and I got busy in the kitchen.

"Okay!" I said. "We need to get the fire going so we can cook dinner." I struck one of the long matches against a rock, and lit the paper that we had packed under the wood. After a few blows, we had a good fire going.

Suddenly, something went terribly wrong. Hot cinders began floating out of the pit, and the crackling flames leapt dangerously close to the ceiling of our newly constructed home. As we watched in disbelief, the dry canvas began to smoke and suddenly burst into flames.

"Hurry," Ernie cried. "Let's get some water."

After struggling to get two buckets of water out to the chicken yard, we managed to douse the fire, but not before a big, black hole had burned through the once white canvas.

We scurried to dismantle the tent, and neatly folded the canvas into a small rectangular bundle. The three of us stood staring at it in disbelief.

"How could this have happened?" we mumbled to each other. We never meant to harm anything. We just wanted to have a little fun with the great canvas.

We were filled with panic. Mama Nettie, Dad, and Pappy would all be home soon, and we would be in big trouble. We felt even worse because we had disobeyed Mama Nettie by leaving the front yard. We had disobeyed Pappy by entering his room and taking his canvas without permission, and we had committed the greatest crime of all by playing with fire.

Tears flowed down our soot-streaked cheeks as we dug another pit, and we all knelt reverently around the hole as we crammed in every corner of the once beautiful, white canvas. Slowly, we covered the canvas with our remorse.

Just as we expected, no sooner had the old folks entered the gate, than Mama Nettie could tell from the somber look on our faces that something was amiss. It only took Pappy one minute to notice that something was missing from his room, and let's just say that we were reprimanded severely for our actions that day.

"The Three Pioneers" formed a pact, and we vowed never to be disobedient again.

We learned a powerful lesson from the episode of "The Tent," and as we grew in knowledge and wisdom, we knew that God had forgiven us, though I'm not sure that Pappy ever did.

The Great Sawdust Piles

Pearlington, Mississippi is situated on the eastern-most tributary of the Pearl River, about 12 miles upriver from Lake Borgne. The East Pearl River forms the natural boundary between Mississippi and Louisiana on this southernmost tip. The Pearl River splits into five tributaries as it makes its course to the mouth of the Gulf of Mexico. The tributaries are identified by the names East Pearl, East Middle, Middle Middle, West Middle, and the West Pearl.

Mama Adelaide, my great-grandmother, told me that her mother, Harriett Garden, was a full-blooded Choctaw Indian who swam in the river when she was a girl. The Choctaws often dove in the river to retrieve oysters that held beautiful, iridescent pearls, and both the river and the town of Pearlington were named for the abundance of those pearls in that area.

Pearlington is probably the oldest town in southern Mississippi, with the exception of Biloxi. Before the arrival of the white man, Choctaw Indians inhabited the land.

After the arrival of the Frenchman, Simon Favre, many white settlers moved in. The population of the area increased with slaves, too. Favrepoint was later named Gin Road because of the cotton gin located there.

In 1814, the artillery section of Andrew Jackson's army marched to Pearlington, where they took charge of every available boat. The citizens of Pearlington helped Jackson's army to maneuver through unfamiliar waterways to get their guns to the Battle of New Orleans.

The city of Pearlington was incorporated in 1822. Pearlington was once a booming town. Long before bridges were built along the coastline to connect Mississippi to Louisiana, the only way to travel in this region was by riverboat. The city had her own financial institution when Hancock Bank opened its doors in Pearlington on January 8, 1903. The bank was located at the beginning of Gin Road on Highway 604 at the site of the old post office.

Mama Nettie's father, Papa Phillip Peters, had worked on the schooners before becoming a boat captain himself. Mama Nettie told me that there was a terrible storm on the Mississippi-Louisiana coast in October of 1893. Her father was thought to be lost at sea with his cousin, Captain Eli Peters, aboard the schooner Eliza B. after the boat began to take on water in Ship Island Harbor.

When Papa Phillip, Captain Eli, and the two crewmembers went overboard, they all grabbed a floating log, which was part of their cargo. The two crewmembers gave up and drowned, but the two cousins clung to the log as they were driven across the Gulf of Mexico. They eventually washed up on the west coast of Florida some 200 miles away. My great-grandfather was barely alive, but he survived the ordeal and went on to command his own schooner.

When automobiles replaced the horse and buggy, highways and bridges were constructed around the mid 1930s to accommodate them. Soon, boat traffic disappeared except for an occasional fisherman. The large logs that were once floated downriver and transported by the schooners were now hauled to the paper mill on big trucks.

Pearlington was no longer the thriving river port, but things continued to flourish when the bridges went in. Highway 90 ran from Louisiana and ended after it crossed the East Pearl River, and highway 604 began there. It turned sharply to the left, and passed straight through the heart of Pearlington. Back then, this was the only route to the Mississippi Gulf Coast, and the Greyhound Bus passed there, too. Highway 604 ran from Pearlington to Westonia, which is now the junction of Highway 607.

Westonia was once called Possum Walk. Uncle Bud wrote in his book that when the last of the known Choctaw Indians left Pearlington in 1902, a single Choctaw, called Indian Joe, remained in Possum Walk.

Years later, around 1936, a shortcut was constructed to make an extension of Highway 90 to connect New Orleans to the Mississippi Gulf Coast. Once that road went in, Pearlington's through traffic stopped abruptly.

The big business in Pearlington and the surrounding communities was logging, and nearly all of the men were loggers or mill workers. Simon Favre's grandson, Captain John Favre, and John's brother-in-law, Captain John Poitevant, ran a prosperous lumber business in the late 1800s.

The Poitevant & Favre Lumber Company owned three sawmills in Pearlington, but two were destroyed by fire in December of 1879. They eventually sold out their sawmill holdings, and by the 1940s, Mr. Sam Whitfield owned most or all of the land where the Pearlington loggers went to cut the tall, straight pines for the pulpwood business. Mr. Whitfield also owned the twenty big trucks used by the loggers to haul the wood to the paper mill.

The loggers worked long, hard, backbreaking hours because they were paid by the truckload for the timber. Back then, they used axes to down the trees and handsaws to cut the massive trunks. Their jobs became easier when hydraulic lifts and gas-powered saws were introduced. However, many of the old loggers suffered in later years with various ailments due to years of lifting the heavy logs, and the constant vibration of the big buzz saws.

When I was a girl, Mr. Charlie Russ owned the saw-mill in Pearlington, and it was located on the river. By day, the mill was a busy place. A continuous line of trucks pulled in during the afternoon hours to unload the giant tree trunks. The great saws screamed and groaned as the logs were forced along the hungry teeth of their blades. Crusty, bark-edged boards emerged from the front of the saw, and a thick cloud of orange sawdust spewed from the great saw's underbelly.

The sawdust was piled high on the riverbank. There were two large hills, which stood at least two stories high. Those hills seemed as high as mountains to our tiny legs as we climbed to the top and ran down the opposite side, as fast as we could.

Playing on the sawdust piles was certainly the most exciting fun to be found in Pearlington. There was only one thing wrong with that. We were not allowed on the river, and we were definitely prohibited from going on the sawdust piles.

"Stay away from that river," Mama Nettie said. "And don't ever go on those sawdust piles. The sawdust forms sink holes, and you kids could be sucked in. You will suffocate and die if that happens."

We all understood what suffocation and death meant, but for the life of me, I could not imagine what a sinkhole looked like. I was certain that we would recognize one if we should ever run across it, and by some miracle, we never did.

I shall always believe what the old folks said. "God takes care of babies and fools!" Thank goodness that we fit into both categories.

Though I don't recall going often, there were a few occasions when the desire for something different got the best of us, and we would sneak off to the river to indulge in an afternoon romp on the great sawdust piles.

When I was about six years old, we were playing outside one summer afternoon. Ernie, Art and I were bored, and we were trying to think of something a little more adventurous to do.

"I've got it," one of us shouted. "Let's go to the river!"

It never did take much to convince the others once one of us had a good idea, so without too much consideration, "The Three Pioneers" headed out.

Things were different when we were young. No one worried about their children, as we are forced to do today. Everyone in the neighborhood watched out for each other. We were instructed to never talk to strangers, and if anyone looked suspicious, an alarm went out throughout the entire community.

No one had telephones, but there was a special whistle that the old folks used to alert each other. Strangers hardly ever came to Pearlington anyway, except for an occasional gypsy family selling wooden chairs from the back of their pickup truck. We were deathly afraid of the gypsies, because we heard that they stole small children. So when the gypsies made their rounds in the springtime, we did not venture far from the safety of the front yard.

It was normal for us to take long hikes, or to go off on an exploration trip deep into the woods. During the summer months, we had chores to do in the mornings between watering the garden and feeding the ducks and chickens, but our afternoons were free to do whatever we liked. It was not uncommon for us to be gone for hours, but we always told Mama Nettie where we were headed. On this particular afternoon, however, we just slipped off from the yard without a word because in our tiny, young minds, it was a far greater sin to lie than to disobey by going to the river.

The sawmill had closed down for the day, and there was only the sound of laughter as we ran up one side and rolled down the other of the great sawdust piles. We scrambled about like three dynamos, round and around, up and down.

Time flew by, and we realized that it was getting late. We were worried that Mama Nettie might be looking for us by now, and we were just about to leave when we caught sight of a man in a small boat. He was riding slowly along the opposite bank. As he passed, we all waved and shouted from the top of the sawdust pile closest to the riverbank. The East Pearl River is about two hundred feet wide at that point, so the boatman was out of earshot, but he waved back to us. We continued to stare at him until he disappeared around a bend in the river. As we watched, we each expressed our fantasies about having a boat of our own.

We turned to leave again when we saw the boat coming back. Once again, we let out a frenzy of waves and yells. The man waved again and passed us. We continued to watch as he ran his boat under the drawbridge and made a circle to come back. This time, however, instead of returning along the far side of the river, he pointed the bow toward the sawdust pile and headed straight for us.

Suddenly, our glee changed to reluctance. We knew everyone in town, and as the boat came closer, we realized that this man was definitely a stranger. He looked thin, and he had long, oily, chestnut-colored hair that whipped about his face in the late afternoon breeze. He smiled at us with yellow teeth, and I noticed that several of his front teeth were missing. The only thing pleasant about him was the blue of his eyes. Years later when I read about Ichibod Crane in "The Legend of Sleepy Hollow" I would always picture this man's face.

We stood there atop the sawdust pile until he reached the dock.

"Hello!" he yelled.

"Hello!" we each replied in unison.

"You kids live around here?" he asked.

"Yes sir!" we replied.

"Well, you three look like nice kids. I bet that you would like to go for a boat ride."

"We're not supposed to talk to strangers," I said.

"Now don't you go worrying about me. My name is Mr. Reinhardt, and I have eight kids of my own. It's all right. We'll just take a little ride, and you'll be home before you know it."

It didn't take long before we had tossed our worries to the wind, and off we went into that boat. Oh! Did I forget to mention that none of us knew how to swim? We took a little spin up the river and circled back, but instead of taking us to the dock, he took a right turn through an outlet that ran across the next three tributaries of the Pearl River.

We were really worried now.

"We need to get home!" Ernie whimpered.

"Oh, don't worry, we won't be long," he replied.

The Pearl River runs down from northern Mississippi as a single artery, but before it reaches the Gulf, it splits into five sections like the prongs of a fork. Pearlington is located on the first prong, or the easternmost sector.

Back in the 1860s, Simon Favre's grandsons had built the thriving lumber business along the tributaries of the Pearl. Years later, J. A. Weston bought them out, and dug a canal perpendicular to the five tributaries to connect them. The lumber companies floated the timber down the river to sawmills, that were located in Pearlington and Logtown, Mississippi, and Bogalusa, Louisiana.

We were on that canal for what seemed an eternity. Finally, Mr. Reinhardt pulled up to a small houseboat that was docked under the West Pearl River Bridge. We had traveled nearly five miles from home. He tied the boat up to the railing of the houseboat and climbed out.

"Come on aboard." he said, and he pulled us up one-by-one, and stood us on the deck of the houseboat. "How would you kids like some hot chocolate and oranges?" he asked.

This man was strange, I thought. Even I knew that oranges didn't go well with hot chocolate. Where were the cookies?

"No, I don't want any, I want to go home," I said.

I always did have a vivid imagination, and a thousand fears ran through my mind as I stood on the deck of that houseboat. Will this man kill us and throw our bodies in the river for the alligators to eat? Would he drown us before the gators got to us? Maybe he was just riding around in his boat looking for three pick-a-ninnies to poison with hot chocolate. He insisted that we all drink up, so I downed the fatal liquid.

"We really need to get home now," said Ernie. Finally, Mr. Reinhardt decided to take us back.

"Finish your chocolate, and we can get going."

The toothless boatman pulled up to shore, and we jumped out of the boat. Our hearts were filled with elation to once again have our feet firmly planted on solid ground.

We turned to run, but he yelled, "Hey, maybe I should go home with you kids so I can tell your mama where you've been."

The words were frozen in my throat, but we all managed to say, "No, that's okay."

"But I insist," replied the nuisance.

"Really, we'll be just fine," we answered, and off we ran as fast as our trembling legs would carry us.

We made it back to the house and peeked into the kitchen to see Mama Nettie busy preparing supper. No one spoke a word, but we were happy to be back in the safe, secure comfort of the old house.

Shortly after Ernie had become a family member, a room was added to the right of the living room to create a bedroom for the two of us. The new addition filled in the open space, and the house was now shaped into a perfect rectangle. There was now a door that opened onto the side yard from our room.

We heard a knock at the side door, and peering through the screen was none other than that crazy Mr. Reinhardt. "How did he find us?" we wondered. We calmly walked through the kitchen and took off out the back door, but a few minutes later, Mama Nettie called.

"Ernie, Gail, and Art, come here please!"

We walked into the living room, bracing to face the consequences.

"Do you children know this gentleman?" Grandmother asked. We stood with heads bowed, staring at our bare feet.

"Yes, Mama!" We nodded.

"Well, Mr. Reinhardt was kind enough to stop by Miss Fryeburg's store to inquire about you, and he came over just to let me know what good and well behaved children you are. Now go ahead and thank Mr. Reinhardt for the nice boat ride, and the hot chocolate and oranges that he gave you on his houseboat. He told me that he never would have seen you if you wouldn't have been waving to him from the sawdust pile, down by the river."

Before we could react, the dead silence was pierced by the sickening sound of splintering wood and shattering glass. Mr. Reinhardt had decided to perch his toothless hide on Mama Nettie's treasured, glass-topped coffee table. That table had belonged to Papa Phillip's sister, Sefronia. Mama Nettie lovingly called her aunt, "Godmother," and she loved that table almost as much as she loved us. Mr. Reinhardt now sat on the floor with his feet flapping in the air. His toothless grin had turned to a grimace as he attempted to pull himself up from the tangled rubble.

For a few seconds, we all stood frozen in time. I was surely praying that the clock would turn back, and that none of these things had ever happened. The great fun on the sawdust piles had just turned into my worst nightmare. Suddenly, I was hoping that the poison in that hot chocolate would kick in right now. I knew that dying could not possibly be worse than what was yet to come.

Mr. Reinhardt began apologizing for the broken table, and offered to pay for the damages, but Mama Nettie said in her ever soft, gentle voice, "No sir, that's perfectly alright. I thank you for being so kind to my children, but I think it's about time for you to leave now!" We continued to stand there, staring at the mess in disbelief.

Mama Nettie began to cry. "This is going to hurt me more than it will hurt you," she said. One by one, she placed us over her knee and spanked us with Dad's old strap. She repeated the same words to each of us.

"I told you never to go to the river. I told you never to play on the sawdust piles, and I told you never to speak to strangers and because of your disobedience, Godmother's table has been destroyed."

She delivered a blow for every other word she spoke. When she was done, she hugged us all to her chest, and the silent tears streamed down her beautiful face.

She was right! The pain of the spanking has long since been forgotten, but even 50 years later, I still remember the pain in her face. And years later, I understood, too, that she just wanted to keep us safe.

Within six months, we would meet the destroyer, Mr. Reinhardt, once again. We would soon learn, also, that he was too poor to pay for that table, and he probably came to our house that infamous evening in the hope of getting an invitation to dinner.

School Days

Summer had long since passed, and we were all back in school. Art was four years old, and I was five, when we attended first grade together in a tiny, makeshift classroom that was set up in the back of Holmes Chapel United Methodist Church. The last three pews were pushed together, and a few desks were added to the small space. It was there that I learned to read, and write my first alphabets.

That church still stands today on the corner of Highway 604 and Whites Road. I mentioned before that my grandmother always prayed for things that she wanted, and the beautification of Holmes Chapel Church was always the first thing on her prayer list. That prayer list was scribbled on a big piece of cardboard, and it hung reverently on her bedroom wall. Though she never lived to see the improvements to the church come to pass, I believe that the remarkable changes came about through her years of intercession.

Mama Nettie made my pretty school dresses from the cloth of flour sacks. We always had a nickel to buy a new pencil or a big apple from one of the crates sitting out front of Mr. John Bayer's store. I can still remember the smell of the apples. They were individually wrapped in purple tissue paper, and I would keep the paper to sniff the fragrance long after the juicy apple was consumed.

When I started second grade, Ernie had joined the family, and we were all bussed to the neighboring community of Logtown. I can remember being excited about going to school and excited about learning. I loved to read and felt a desire to know everything.

I don't recall too many details of that year of my life at Logtown School. The school was called the pillbox. Oh, it was small all right, but it was really named for the hundreds of goat droppings that were scattered about the porch and playground every morning. I think every goat herd in Logtown bedded down at the elementary school each night, and did their business.

One event that does stick out in my memory was the sight of our teacher fainting in the classroom. I'd seen a few corpses in church at funeral services, and Miss Nearly sure looked plenty dead to me. It was quite a traumatizing experience to see the teacher laid out on the floor as stiff as a tree stump. I overheard the old folks discussing the incident one night, and Mama Nettie said that Miss Nearly wasn't dead, she was just pregnant. I didn't understand what that meant, but I figured it must have been something like dead, because I never saw her again. I decided right then that I would never be a schoolteacher.

You are probably getting the picture by now that I was one scared cowgirl. I was afraid of the dark and afraid of shadows. I was afraid of the thunder and afraid of the silence. I was afraid of the living and afraid of the dead. I was afraid of the cows, the geese and the spiders, but the thing that still petrifies me most is the sight of a snake. It does not matter what shape or color.

Though I did bold things at times, there was no bravery in me! I was struck with fear throughout all of my childhood, and things didn't get better until I was about 25 years old. All of that anxiety was more than likely due to my overactive imagination.

I always had to logic things out when I was small. I remember a particular incident that happened when I was about four years old. Art and I were home alone with Dad, and I was eating a succulent orange when I happened to swallow a seed. I stopped eating to think. Let's see. An orange seed grows a root, and from the root comes a tree, and from the tree grows branches, and I began to feel the explosion of a giant trunk deep inside of me. I panicked and started running through the house, screaming. Dad chased me through a couple of rooms, and grabbed me by the back of my collar.

"What's wrong, are you hurt?" he demanded. I couldn't speak, for the fear choked me. At that moment, I thought it was a limb.

"I swallowed an orange seed," I screamed. "Now I'm going to die because the tree will burst me open." Dad held back his laughter and looked down at me with a stern face.

"Now you hush that squalling! No tree can grow without fertilizer, so I think you'll be just fine."

With reluctant relief, I managed to calm down, but I vowed that I wouldn't take any more chances with seeds.

The Barber Chair

We were always inventing new games, and my favorite was "Barber Chair." Each child took a turn playing the chair. One of us had to lie on our back, and bend our knees while holding our feet up high to form the seat of the chair. Someone else would sit in the chair for a haircut. When the barber was done, the chair would spring forward with a snap, and the lucky recipient would go flying through the air.

One evening, we were all sitting in the living room after supper. There was a knock at the front door, and Mama Nettie went to answer. We could hear the sound of voices in the front bedroom as the old folks settled down for a long conversation with the visitors.

"Let's go outside!" someone suggested, and off we went out the back door to strike up a game of "Barber Chair." We each took turns playing the chair, but on my second time around to get my haircut, I was hurled through the air and landed smack in the middle of the trash bin. I fell on a tin can, and cut a big gash in my left hand at the top of my thumb. The blood gushed, and Ernie's eyes stretched as she stared at me. I was afraid, because we should never have left the living room.

"Don't tell!" I pleaded. We went back to the living room, and I sat down and tried to squeeze my dripping hand between my thighs.

"We must tell Mama Nettie," Ernie said, and she ran off to turn me in.

My grandmother came hurriedly and took me into her room. She tore strips of white cloth and held some to my hand real tight, but she could not get the bleeding to subside.

"Go call Mama Adelaide!" she yelled to Art and Ernie. Within a few minutes, they were all back. Mama Adelaide took a look at my hand and asked for a lantern and a fishing pole. She went out to the shed and twisted a thick mass of spider webs around the tip of the cane pole.

Mama Adelaide came back to the house, and I started screaming the minute I caught sight of what she held in her hand. Mama Nettie and Dad held me down while my great-grandmother pressed the sticky webs to my wound. She poured alcohol over the webs and bound them tightly to my hand with strips of the white cloth. I felt no pain, but I continued to weep for hours because I didn't want the creepy webs attached to my hand. I knew that spiders would eventually come crawling out from my bandage.

If this had happened today I would have taken about ten stitches, but the old remedy did the trick. We now know that spider webs help the blood clotting mechanism and they have an antibiotic property too. Back then, my great-grandmother used the medicinal remedies that her Choctaw mother had passed down to her. Only a thin line remains as a faint reminder of my late evening visit to the barbershop.

Treating my injury with spider webs was not the only cure that Mama Nettie used on us. Harriet Garden passed down cures from her Indian culture, and her daughter, Mama Adelaide, passed them on to my grandmother.

If we had a cold with a bad cough, Mama Nettie brewed tea by boiling lemons, honey and pine needles. If someone had a high fever, she would stuff the leaves of the elderberry plant into a pillowcase and lay us on top. She then wrapped us tightly in a blanket, and then she would retire to the armless rocking chair where she rocked us until the fever broke. The fresh green leaves of the elderberry plant would turn brown from the body heat, and according to my grandmother, the plant's medicinal powers pulled the fever from our bodies.

I burned my left leg one summer day when I pulled a pot of boiling beans from the stove. I was scalded from the knee to the top of my foot. After the blisters drained, a thick layer of skin fell away, and my raw flesh was so painful that I could not stand to expose it to the light of day.

Mama Nettie kept the shades pulled in Pappy's old room, and I stayed in bed for more than a week. She came in several times a day to apply one of her homemade poultices to my leg. I remember seeing her put baking soda into a bowl, but I don't know the other ingredients that she used to make the cool paste. After two weeks, Mama Nettie gave me Pappy's crutches to use, and I started going outside for a while. When I returned to school in September, there was no sign of my injury, and the severe burn left no scars.

I was about as accident-prone as they come, and I had more than my share of cuts, scrapes, insect bites and childhood diseases. I was real lucky to have a grandmother who knew how to fix all of my ills and injuries.

Shame, Shame

I tried to be an obedient child because I wanted my folks to be proud of me. Unfortunately, my curious nature was my constant downfall. For the most part though, I did manage to do the right thing. However, I still feel guilty when I think of the one time in my life that I accidentally let my grandmother see a false side of me, and it still makes me feel ashamed to this day.

Mama Nettie took care of my first cousin, Janice, too. I was too young to remember the circumstances or the date of her arrival in the household, but Janice was old enough to walk. Mama Nettie said that there was a terrible rainstorm the night that her mother, Phyllis, came to take her back to New Orleans.

"Please, don't take the baby out in this weather," Mama Nettie begged. A few days later, Janice came down with a high fever, and she contracted polio. Afterwards, she passed many years in surgery and physical therapy to correct her right leg, which had been ravished by the disease.

After her illness, Janice was absent from the country for years, and she had a clear phobia for every farm creature. I guess I was a little envious of her. She was an only child, and she had been naturally pampered and spoiled due to her devastating illness. When no one was around, she would pinch or bite us, and run screaming to Mama Nettie that we had hit her.

In the summer of 1954, Janice came to Pearlington with a full set of white Samsonite luggage, with the makeup case included, and each suitcase had a white, pearl handle. Her luggage was filled with new clothes, and lots of new shoes. I thought that they were very expensive, and I had never seen so much luxury.

Sure, we had everything that we needed, but most of my dresses were made from flour sacks, and I had only two pairs of shoes. I had often thumbed through the Sears & Roebuck catalogue and wished for one of those pretty jumpers that zipped up the front. Janice had one in almost every color: pink, yellow, green and blue. This made my brownish-green eyes turn emerald with envy.

Janice and I were always fussing about whose hair was the longest, or the thickest, and she usually won the argument. No one dared to inflict any physical harm upon her because Mama Nettie always told us how sick she was. We all felt sorry for her, and we would kneel with Mama Nettie every night to pray for Janice when she was going through those bad periods of surgery and rehabilitation.

However, all of my feelings of pity were quickly diminished about ten minutes after Janice's arrival every summer. So, I never missed a chance to toss one of the fat, red hens her way when we went out to feed the chickens every morning. She would squeal and cry. At least seeing the fear in her eyes when she turned to flee from the chicken yard gave me some joy of payback for all of those bites and pinches.

We always played down the road under a big oak tree that sat in the middle of Hancock Street, just across Whites Road. Janice and I got into a squabble one afternoon while playing under that oak tree. She darted to run, and I reached out to grab her. As I lurched for her, I accidentally ripped the seam on the shorts of her new jumper. She began to cry, and insisted that her mother would spank her because her clothes were torn.

I decided to show off in front of the other kids, so I mimicked some of the older girls by putting my hands on my hips. "Well, you can go ahead and cry baby, because I don't care about your old jumpsuit. Cry baby, cry baby," I sang and I swayed my hips from side to side.

To my dismay, it turned out that I had not only put on a show for the other kids, Mama Nettie, her uncle, Etienne Maxson, whom we called Uncle Bud, and Mama Adelaide were sitting on Uncle Bud's front porch, and they had all witnessed the entire thing.

"I am so disappointed in you," Mama Nettie told me. I never thought that you would act like that. The street walkers on Rampart Street in New Orleans act that way, but not my little girl."

I held my head low, and the tears rolled down my cheeks. I couldn't find the words to explain that it was just an act. I wanted to say that the person under the oak tree wasn't really me, but instead, I stood with my lips clamped tightly.

Nothing could have affected me more than knowing that I had hurt my grandmother. Though I'm certain that I did things later on that may have pained her more, this one little event taught me a great lesson. I have never been able to offend anyone like that again, and fortunately, as we grew we all forgot our childish whims and became great friends.

Chapter IX

The Happiest Time of Our Lives

Life on the Farm

Dad raised pigs and a few cows in addition to the chickens, ducks and geese. Caring for the pigs and cows was not part of our daily chores, because my grandparents feared we would be bitten or trampled.

That eternal curiosity of mine kept me in trouble, and I still carry a scar on my right thigh from a goose bite. I just wanted to rub an egg, and after biting a chunk out of me, the mother goose tried to flay me to death with her massive wings. Dad heard my screams and ran out to rescue me. He laughed as he picked me up and chased the goose away.

"That goose whipped you good, eh!"

My feelings were hurt to think that he was making fun of me. "She tried to kill me," I whimpered.

I was afraid of the cows, too, because they were so large, but I loved to run behind the chickens to make them scatter about the yard. When we fed them, I would toss the corn close to my feet and giggle as the hungry birds picked at my bare toes to retrieve their meal.

Dad borrowed a mule from his neighbor, Mr. Elijah Peters, and he plowed the fields for planting. When the rows were neatly banked, Dad walked along and poked holes in the dirt. Art and I would drop in a seed or the joint of a sweet potato vine; pour in a little can full of water and fill the hole with soil.

It was our job to water the newly planted garden daily. We would make the long journey back and forth to the water pump that was located behind the house. When our buckets were full, we had to carry them through the chicken yard to get out to the fields again. We were always happy to see the arrival of summer, which brought the afternoon showers, because that meant we'd get a watering break.

Mama Nettie would give us a chunk of dough and let us make biscuits while she prepared breakfast. She would let us watch while she rolled out the crust for her special pies, or beat the fluffy egg whites for her creamy cake frosting. Our grandparents made sure to teach us as much as they could, and we were always anxious to know how every-thing worked.

Every November, some of the men from town came to help, and they would slaughter one or two fat pigs. Fires were built under big, cast iron pots out in a corner of the yard, and one by one the giant creatures were put to sleep. The men cut their throats to let the blood drain out, and then they dipped the pigs into hot, boiling water. The animals were then placed on a clean sheet of tin, and everyone gathered around to scrape the gray, outer skin until a clean white layer emerged.

Holes were cut through the bones in the pig's hind legs, and a long wooden rod was extended from one leg to the other. Great hooks hung from ropes that were tied to thick tree limbs, and the hooks were connected to each end of the rod. The men pulled the ropes to hoist the pig up, and a tub was placed underneath. The animals great bellies were split open, and the internal organs would tumble out into the tub.

Everything from the inside of the pigs was placed into different enameled pans, and the women came to get them. Nothing was wasted. Even the bladder was blown up, tied off and left to dry in the sun. It would eventually make a basketball for us. The ball was a smelly thing that produced an almost metallic sound as it bounced, but we had lots of fun with it.

The pigs were cut into various pieces. Hams were hung in the smokehouse, and most of the meat was salted down and placed in wooden crates. There were cracks in the crates to allow the liquids to seep out. Dad would add more salt to the crates during the long period that it took for the meat to be properly cured. The thick skin was fried to make cracklings (pork rinds to Northerners or chicharrones to Latinos), and the lard was saved for frying and biscuit making. Mama Nettie made soap by cooking lard mixed with lye.

The process of killing and butchering the animals was a bit gruesome for tots, but the excitement of the occasion outweighed the sight of blood. The yard was bustling with people, and it was a busy time for everyone. The women were in the kitchen separating and butchering the meat and preparing a big meal of fresh pork. The men laughed heartily as they sipped anise-flavored moonshine, and warmed their hands around a sparkling fire in the yard.

During the winter months, the men loaded their long shotguns, and they went into the woods to hunt wild ducks, rabbits, squirrels and raccoons. I can still savor the taste of roasted, wild meat, surrounded by baked sweet potatoes on a plate next to a nice mess of steaming turnip greens, a chunk of crusty corn bread, and a hot cup of sassafras tea. Mama Nettie sure could cook!

Meat wasn't the only thing in abundance. We ate lots of fresh fish. Dad went out at night with his friends to the river, and there they threw their great nets. The Pearl River empties into the Gulf of Mexico, so there was a good variety of fresh and saltwater fish in the river. The ample catches of ground mullet, perch, croakers and trout were cleaned and cooked or stored in thick wooden barrels that were filled with salt brine. We had great fish fries, and the rest was divided up among the neighbors.

We gathered eggs, and Mama Nettie would often stew one of our fat hens for Sunday dinner. Though I never did like milk after Art was weaned from the bottle, there was milk in excess from the cows, and Dad made butter in a big, wooden churn. He also made cottage cheese by letting the milk sour, and pouring the clabber into big strainers to let the water drain out.

There was always a summer and a winter garden with fresh tomatoes, greens, potatoes, sweet potatoes, corn, and every variety of beans, squash, pumpkins, watermelons, cucumbers and sugarcane. We picked pears, figs and plums from the fruit trees, and we gathered blackberries, wild grapes (called scuppernongs), and tiny, crabapple-shaped berries (called may hauls) from the woods. The tall stalks of sugarcane were cut in the fall and taken to the mill to make molasses.

There were two mulberry trees in the garden. When the berries hung thick on their branches, we would fetch a cup of cream and sugar from the kitchen, and climb up the tree to enjoy a very fresh desert. We always descended from the tree with purple clothes, hands and feet.

Mama Nettie canned the vegetables and fruit. She even made preserves from the watermelon rind. Great pots bubbled on the stove at harvest time, and she would line up hundreds of mason jars on the counter. The jars were filled and sealed with a thick layer of hot wax.

Mama Nettie and Dad gave fresh meat, fish, eggs, milk, molasses, fruit and vegetables to their four adult children and all of the neighbors. They never forgot to include the widows and the elderly folks in the community, and we still had jars stacked in every cabinet and under every bed.

Pig Cakes

Dad treated his animals well, and the pigs were no exception. Although we were too small to care for the big animals, we did take great joy in sharing the pigs' dinner.

Dad used two big barrels to mix the pigs' food. He put water in the barrels, and added wheat grain, corn, table scraps and day-old bread and cakes. Those cakes were the objects of our attention.

Twice a week, the bread man came out from New Orleans and left two large brown paper sacks at the front gate. We always waited on delivery days to be sure that we got to the sacks before Dad did. We would drag the four-foot high sacks to a safe spot and empty the contents. There was always an abundance of cakes from the Marita Bakery to bring tears of joy to our young eyes.

We each had our favorites, but I loved the seven-layer coconut cream and the chocolate layer cakes. There were lemon cream and angel food cakes, jellyrolls and every delight that one could imagine. We would each come out with at least five cakes, and we ate cake until we threw up. The bags also contained long loaves of French bread, but we always left those for the pigs. We managed to get away with this for a short while, but soon Dad caught on and that was the end of our pig cake sprees.

The Sugarcane Mill

Every aspect of our young lives was filled with new learning experiences, but one of the things that I will always treasure is the memory of our trips to the sugarcane mill.

Mr. Oscar White lived in the area, and Dad called him every year to come with his long wagon to take the sugarcane to the mill. The mill was located about 20 miles away in Gainesville, Mississippi.

Mr. White's long wagon was drawn by a beautiful white horse named Lightning. Lightning was the kind of horse that you'd expect a prince to ride when he went out to court his fair maiden.

Blinders shielded the horse's eyes, and when he started to whinny, Mr. White would place his large hands on the horse's head and whisper something in his ear. He seemed like a giant of a man to us, and he probably stood over six feet tall. His skin was black, and he had a big shaved head. I never heard him say a word, and if we asked him a question, he would usually just nod his shiny head and smile.

Mr. White stood grooming his horse while Dad and his helpers piled the freshly cut sugarcane stalks high onto the wagon bed. When the wagon was loaded, we headed off to Gainesville. Mr. White let the three of us ride up on the long seat of the wagon, and Dad and Mama Nettie followed us in the old truck. We couldn't have guessed in a million years that Mr. White would be our new great-grandfather one day when he married Mama Adelaide in 1960.

Mr. Percy Peters owned the sugarcane mill. Though Mr. Percy had the same last name as my grandmother, they were not related. We pulled into the yard and were greeted by a large family of women and children. The cane was quickly unloaded and placed near a conveyor belt. When everyone was ready, a mule was harnessed to a device resembling a "merry go round," and one of Mr. Peters' sons tugged at the bridle while another boy patted the mule's right flank. Slowly, the stubborn mule began to walk around in a circle, and the rusty gears of the mill creaked into motion. Sugarcane began moving up a conveyor belt about ten feet from the ground towards a big press.

The machine had giant rollers made of iron, and they began to suck up the cane. The light, green juice was funneled down to the holding tables as the cane was squeezed through the heavy wheels of the press. The tables were made of metal, and they stood about four feet off the ground. There were metal walls around the edge of the tables to contain the sweet juice. When the juice started flowing down, Mr. Peters and the other adults lit large fires under each section of the holding table.

The ladies stood along the table to stir the bubbling juices with long wooden spoons. They continued to stir the translucent, green fluid until it started to thicken and began turning light brown in color.

"Come here, girlie, have a taste!" said Mr. Peters. I ran over to him and took a sip from the big wooden spoon. "Is that good?" he asked.

"Yes Sir!" I replied shyly, and ran off to play with the other children.

The syrup began to thicken and turn dark brown, and Mr. Peters and his family started filling shiny, silver cans with the thick, dark molasses. They placed half of the filled cans in Dad's truck, and they kept the other half. When they were done, we all sat down on blankets under big shade trees to eat lunch with Mr. Peters and his family. Mr. Peters said a blessing, and we enjoyed the cool lemonade and fried chicken that the ladies had prepared for us.

On the way home I asked, "Dad, why did we leave half of the molasses at Mr. Peters' house?"

"Well," said Dad, "we left half to pay Mr. Peters for making the molasses for us. We wouldn't have molasses if he wouldn't have had the mill, and that's what you call bartering." With a full stomach, and the excitement of the long day, I went fast to sleep as we made the journey home from the sugarcane mill.

The Reinhardts Move Next Door

"The Three Pioneers" were busy studying, and eagerly anticipating the Christmas holiday season. One evening when we got home from Logtown School, we learned that a family had moved in down the block.

Mama Nettie and Dad lived on a dead end street. There was an empty field to the left of the house, and a single house stood at the end of the road. We knew the house intimately because many transient families had moved in, and out, over the years. The house was old. It had four large rooms and no running water. Naked floorboards were exposed, and you could see outside through the cracks during the day. There must have been an outhouse, but when you're six or seven years old, that's just not a thing that sticks in your memory. We all feared the big, gaping holes, so for us outhouses were something to be avoided as much as humanly possible.

Early the following Saturday morning, we were up at the crack of dawn to get our chores done because we were anxious to get out to investigate the new neighbors. By 9:00 a.m. we had fed the chickens, oiled the furniture and washed up the breakfast dishes. We were now free, and off we went.

We soon learned that the family was none other than that of the infamous Mr. Reinhardt, the "boatman" from the sawdust piles adventure, and the murderer of Mama Nettie's prized table. His wife looked just like him, tall and lanky, with oily, brown hair and a mouthful of bad teeth. There were five girls, two small boys about Art's age, and a baby boy who was about 10 months old. The girls, to Ernie's and my delight, were about our age or a little older, and we struck up an immediate friendship. Ernie and I loved combing the girl's long hair, and we would take them down to our house to wash their hair with Mama Nettie's Prell Shampoo.

Mr. Reinhardt did tell the truth about one thing: he had eight children. He had dropped his family off and disappeared. Maybe he was off working someplace, but we never saw him around the house.

Mama Nettie and Dad soon became the guardian angels of this poor family. Oh, don't get me wrong, we were poor too, only we didn't know it. We had everything in abundance, and my kind and loving grandparents always shared what they had with the less fortunate. We didn't consider anything strange when we saw familiar canned goods, milk, fresh fruit and vegetables from our house in their kitchen. I did note, too, that the extra bag of pig bread that Dad now ordered always showed up in their kitchen.

"God has blessed us, and it is the right thing for us to do to help others, because this is what the Lord expects of us." Mama Nettie always said.

We learned a lot of things from my grandparents. They taught us to be kind, caring, and considerate to others, but most of all, they taught us the true meaning of love.

The Season of Christmas

Mama Nettie was busy baking cakes and pies and making chocolate fudge and white divinity candy. We peeled pecans for her special fruitcakes, candy, and stuffed dates. We went into the woods with Dad and found a ten-foot cedar, and Mama Nettie hummed Christmas carols as we hung garland and bubble lights around our Christmas tree.

We had turned the pages of the Sears Catalog for months, and had picked out Pappy's socks and suspenders, Dad's shirt and tie, and a girdle and a beautiful dress for our grandmother. Our letter had gone out to Santa with a list of things that we hoped for.

"I'm going to look mighty funny walking down the street in just socks and suspenders!" Pappy said, and we all had a good laugh.

On Christmas Eve, the house was filled with the odor of baking, and by evening at least eight baskets sat on the kitchen table, ready for delivery. Mama Nettie had packed a baked hen with stuffing, a fruitcake, a pack of candy, and a sweet potato pie into each basket. Those sweet potato pies were my favorite. Mama Nettie made them with lots of thick cream and eggs, sugar, cinnamon and a dash of nutmeg. When it was dark, we loaded the baskets into the truck and headed out on our mission to play Santa for some of the old folks in the community. Art and I carried a basket to each door, and when they answered, we handed it to them.

"Merry Christmas!" we shouted, and before they could say anything, we'd turn, and run back to the truck.

We were too young to understand the real significance of this single act back then, yet it is but another one of the things that will stand out in my heart forever. Years later, I found myself repeating the same tradition. It is the one thing that has made my heart eternally tender.

Dad waited for my mother's oldest brother, Uncle Gene, to arrive from New Orleans, and around 9:00 p.m. they joined a couple of other men from town to go out Christmas caroling.

On Christmas morning we were up at first light, anxious to open the presents. I had my doll, and Ernie had her gifts. Art had his bike, and everyone was happy to be alive. The house was filled with the odor of gunpowder as we reloaded the little red spools and fired rounds from our cap guns.

Though Mama Nettie and Dad were raising Ernie, they made certain that her mother got to see her whenever she could. Her mom always came loaded down with new clothes and lots of gifts, and this Christmas was no exception.

Mama Nettie had cooked throughout the night, and there was a long table filled with everything that you could imagine. There were mincemeat, apple, sweet potato, and lemon meringue pies, fruitcakes, pound cakes, chocolate cakes, chocolate fudge, white divinity candy, stuffed dates, and ambrosia made from apples, oranges, bananas and nuts. She made her special pineapple-coconut cake with creamy, white frosting that was made from fluffy egg whites and Karo Syrup. A baked turkey was ready, and all the garnishes were prepared for a Christmas feast.

During the course of the day, at least 35 family members and friends would sit down to enjoy dinner, and a non-ending stream of neighbors and visitors would stop by to sample the many goodies on the pastry table.

We sat around the breakfast table after everyone had opened their gifts, and Dad thanked God for our many blessings. He always concluded his long prayers with the same words. "Bless my sister in a distant land."

Dad said the blessing before every meal, but Sunday morning breakfast was always a special occasion. The prayers were extra long. We each had to recite a Bible verse, and we always closed the little prayer session with the same hymn, *At the Cross.*

On this Christmas morning, we waited impatiently to hear the last "amen." After singing the hymn as we did every Sunday morning, we downed our Christmas oatmeal.

It was time to go to church. We all went to Holmes Chapel. Everyone was excited about church this Christmas morning, because we all had practiced our speeches for the children's program.

Ernie tied the sash of my new dress, and Dad made a knot in Art's new bow tie. We lived only a short walk from the church, so we grabbed our coats and skipped across the small puddles, taking great care not to get mud on our new Christmas shoes.

Within a year, I would learn that Art and I were baptized Roman Catholic at birth, and by the time I started third grade, we would attend St. Rose de Lima Catholic School in Bay St. Louis. I followed the Catholic faith, but whenever I visited my grandparents, I attended church with them at the Methodist Church, and then I'd cross the street for Mass at St. Joseph's Catholic Church. Dad always called me a "hard-shell Catholic," and we'd have a good laugh.

It wasn't that simple at school though. Every Monday morning we had to stand and announce to the nuns where we had attended Mass, if they had not spotted us in the

Parish on Sunday. When I told them the truth, that I had attended Holmes Chapel Methodist Church and St. Joseph's Catholic Church in Pearlington, they would harass me and tell me to try to convert my grandparents. I was eight years old, and I made futile attempts to explain to my grandparents why being Catholic was the only way to be saved. Little did those nuns know that my grandparents were already living saints!

Chapter X

Learning to Survive

❀❀❀

The Cold, Cold World

Ernie, Art and I didn't know it at the time, but the world ran on money, too, and there was not much money in our household. My grandparents were fairly self-sufficient. They lived modestly in the old house, and we ate from the garden and the livestock that they raised. They did need money for staples like grits, flour, sugar and coffee, and they purchased the corn, wheat and oat grains to feed the animals.

Dad had three pairs of shoes: black work shoes that were well worn, with strips of leather cut out around the toes to relieve the pressure on his arthritic feet, smelly black, rubber boots that were always covered with cow and chicken manure, and one pair of Italian shoes from Picconi of New Orleans which cost a hundred dollars. He kept his expensive shoes shined, and they were worn to church or funerals only. He owned one black, double-breasted suit, two white shirts and a variety of ties.

Mama Nettie had two or three white uniform dresses. They buttoned up the front with removable buttons. She wore those uniforms whenever she went out to cook a meal in the home of some wealthy neighbor; or when she had to attend a meeting of the Household of Ruth, which was a female version of the all-male Masonic Order. There were several pretty dresses in her armoire. Some she made herself, and others were given to her by the ladies that she worked for. She usually wore slippers around the house, and she had a pair of sandals and one pair of high heels for church.

Dad had not worked for more than 20 years by the time that I was old enough to remember. As a young man, he worked at the brickyard in St. Joe, Louisiana that is near Slidell. During the Depression he held odd jobs as an oyster shucker and a waiter. After his accidental gunshot wound, he got an infection called "osteomyelitis," and had spent months at a time in the hospital over the years. The gunshot wounds never healed, but he survived for 45 years with the bad leg. He even outlived the wise doctor who always told him, "Giles, whatever you do, don't ever let anyone take that leg."

When Mama turned six weeks old, around the end of February in 1930, Mama Nettie bundled up her new baby and rode the Greyhound Bus to New Orleans to visit Dad in Charity Hospital. The nurses took Mama around the ward to show her off.

"My goodness, Mrs. Giles, where on earth did you get such a beautiful, white baby?"

Though Mama would become dark brown-complexioned as she grew older, at birth she was creamy white with straight black hair.

Mama Nettie sat in a chair next to Dad's bed. He had a cast on his right leg that ran from his foot to his hip. They talked for a while about the other children and their little farm.

"How are you doing for money?" Dad asked.

"Now don't you go worrying about a thing. All you have to do is stay here and get well. We will be just fine."

Dad flinched as a wave of pain ran up his leg. "I just hate to see you all alone, Mama. You need help with the new baby and all. Who's going to chop wood for the fire? Who's going to take care of the animals and milk the cows every morning? I know that your Papa Phillip is ailing too much to be of any help to you."

Mama Nettie put her face close to her husband's chest and placed a hand on his cheek. "I tell you not to worry. It's not good for you laying up here all day, fretting about what needs to be done at the house. You just trust in the good Lord. He'll see us through this. Now you finish eating that good dinner I brought you. Visiting hours are almost over."

On the long bus ride home, Mama Nettie prayed quietly. She had never lied to her husband before, but there was no way to tell him that they were just about out of flour and sugar. She dreaded leaving her babies, but there was nothing else to do. The children needed coats and warm socks.

She had found a housekeeping job in Long Beach, Mississippi, and she would be starting in a few days. She would have to sleep on the premises during the week and have Saturdays and Sundays off. Papa Phillip lived with them, but his heart ailment had rendered him too weak to do much of anything.

"Now don't you worry about the kids, Nettie. I can take care of them just fine. Myrtle is old enough to help with the baby, and Gene and Charles can bring in firewood, and tend to the animals. Mr. Cornelius comes by every day or two to chop wood, and Mrs. Cornelius said that she would come over to cook supper and help out around the house.

So you see, there's nothing to worry about. Everything is going to be just fine."

Mama Nettie put her head on her father's shoulder, and they sat in silence and stared at the crackling, yellow and orange flames that roared in the fireplace.

That following Monday morning, Mama Nettie kissed her babies goodbye, and she walked the long road some six miles to Westonia to catch the early bus. She tried to enjoy the ride, but her mind was filled with apprehension about what was ahead, and what she had left behind.

Mrs. Wiley was the mistress of the house. Mr. Wiley was a merchant, and from the looks of things, they had not been affected by the Depression. They had three small children: Elizabeth was ten years old; Andrew was five; and Agnes was three. Mrs. Wiley showed Mama Nettie around the large house, and took her to her quarters just off the kitchen.

"Arnette, I am very particular about my house; I like things done a certain way. I prefer that you do the washing and ironing every Monday and Thursday. Mr. Wiley likes his breakfast ready at seven-thirty every morning. He does not come home for lunch, but I would like for you to prepare a light lunch for the children. The children should be fed, bathed and put to bed before Mr. Wiley gets home."

"I'm out and about most days at lunchtime, but I expect dinner to be ready at six o'clock promptly. I'll stay with you today to show you what I want done in the way of housekeeping. You can stop working at seven-thirty in the evenings, providing that the kitchen is clean and everything is tidy. As we agreed, your stipend will be six dollars per month. Do you have any questions?"

"No, Ma'am," Mama Nettie replied. "I think I understand everything perfectly clear."

"Fine," said Mrs. Wiley. "Well go ahead and put your things away, and I'll give you a few minutes to freshen up before we get started."

The servant's room was small, but tastefully done with a twin bed, a chest of drawers, a mirror, a matching armoire and a small table with a comfortable looking armchair. There were two white sheets, a pillowcase, two small towels, and a beautiful quilt folded at the foot of the bed.

Mama Nettie pulled her clothes from her bag and hung the two white uniforms in the closet. She refolded her nightgown, undergarments and stockings and placed them in the drawer, and she laid her comb and hairbrush on top of the chest of drawers. A basin sat on a stand near the sole window, and she laid her toothbrush and a little packet of baking soda on the little shelf under the washstand. The baking soda was used as toothpaste and deodorant.

A heavy, off-white curtain framed the window. The floors were all dark hardwood, and a small rug ran along the side of the bed. Mama Nettie pulled her Bible from her bag and laid it on the table. At least she would have time to read on those lonely nights. The room looked comfortable, but she wished that it were possible to be home, taking care of her own household and family.

"I won't think about it. I have to do whatever it takes to keep us going until Dad comes home," she thought to herself. She made her bed, took one more look around the room, dressed in one of the white uniforms and tied an apron around her waist before stepping out into the kitchen.

Mrs. Wiley was already there. She was thin, and probably stood at least five feet, eight inches tall. She was rather pretty with friendly blue eyes. Only a nose that was a little too long flawed her otherwise beautifully symmetrical face. She wore fine clothes and shoes. Her thick, blond hair was twisted and pinned to form large swirls at the back of her head. She had changed into an old dress and had tied a scarf around her hair.

"Let's have a cup of tea, and you can tell me all about yourself, Arnette," Mrs. Wiley hummed with her southern accent.

"Please Ma'am, everyone calls me Nettie."

"Nettie it is then, and you can call me Miss Angie, but not in the presence of Mr. Wiley. He would be absolutely mortified to know that I allowed a Colored to call me by my first name."

"Fine, Miss Angie it is." The two women burst into laughter. Mama Nettie told her mistress about the children and Dad's injury.

"Well, that's just horrible, Nettie."

They finished their tea, and Miss Angie walked over to a cabinet. "This is where I keep my cleaning things. I use this oil to polish the furniture and the staircase. Grab that broom, and a stack of cloths over there, and we'll go through the chores together."

By nine o'clock, they had cleaned most of the house with the exception of the children's room.

"Come on, Nettie, go get some grits and eggs going, and I'll bring down those two scalawags of mine to meet you. Elizabeth, my oldest, leaves every morning with her papa. He drops her off at school on his way to work. She will be home by three-thirty every afternoon. Lawdy me, she eats like a little sparrow, but she may want milk or a piece of fruit before supper."

"When you're done, I'll show you the laundry room so you can get started with the clothes. Monday will be the worst laundry day, with the sheets and all. I do apologize for all of Mr. Wiley's shirts too, but he likes a fresh one every day. You'll have to cook up some starch for those because he likes them nice and stiff."

Mama Nettie made it through the long day at the Wiley's. She put away the last of the supper dishes and swept the kitchen floor.

Well, I made it through the first day, she thought, while removing her apron. She hung the apron on a hook in the broom closet and retired to her room. She spent an hour or two reading her Bible by the dim light of an oil lantern, and she wrote a long letter to her husband.

By Friday night, she was mighty glad to be going home. Mr. Wiley dropped her off at the bus station in time for her to catch the eight thirty-five bus to Westonia. Mrs. Wiley had loaded her sack down with flour, sugar, a little bag of coffee and some used clothes from her children. When the bus stopped at Westonia it was nearly nine-thirty, and she still had the long, six-mile walk home.

Mama Nettie stepped off the bus and stood there until its lights faded in the distance. The road ahead was as dark as pitch. She threw the heavy sack over her shoulder and headed down the road. There were few automobiles in Pearlington, but whenever she saw the headlights of an oncoming car, she would lie down in the ditch to hide until the car passed. Most of the ditches were filled with cold, murky water, but that was a far better pain to risk rather than what could happen to a beautiful black woman if she'd been spotted alone on a deserted road.

Mama was only a few weeks old when Mama Nettie started working for the Wiley family. Mama Nettie was still bleeding heavily, and her condition did not seem to improve. As she continued her walk home, she was hemorrhaging so badly that the blood was running down her legs and into her shoes. She removed her heavy cotton stockings, and rolled them up to make a temporary sanitary pad until she could get home. Things got much worse, and when Mama Nettie finally decided to see a doctor, she was told that she had to have a hysterectomy.

She continued to work for the Wiley's for eight months. By then, Dad was well enough to come home. Mama Nettie had her surgery, but during the operation a nurse spilled ether on her lip. When the chemical burned her mouth, she jumped, and the doctor punctured her bladder. The surgery and bladder injury took a long time to heal.

Once Mama Nettie did recover, she stayed home and did laundry for well off people to make a few dollars. She baked cakes or pies upon request too. Word soon spread about her good cooking abilities, and many folks had her in to cook holiday meals, and dinners for parties.

Mama Adelaide worked as a midwife for many years, and she taught my grandmother the art of midwifery. Mama Nettie told me that Dr. Shipp was the doctor for the county, and he made rounds to follow up on the patients under the care of the midwives. One night, during a terrible storm, Mama Nettie was summoned to deliver a baby. When she answered the door, she was surprised to see the expectant mother's sisters, because she didn't even know that the young lady in labor was pregnant.

"Please come quick, Miss Nettie, our sister is dying," the two girls cried.

"I'll be right there," Mama Nettie replied. "Make sure that there's lots of hot water, and lots of clean white rags." Mama Nettie closed the door against the wind and blowing rain.

"Dear Lord, why do babies only decide to come into this world in the middle of a storm?" she whispered. She went back to the bedroom and shook Dad's shoulder. "Charlie, I've been summoned to deliver a baby at the Smith's house," she told my grandfather.

"What time is it?" Dad asked.

"It's nearly two in the morning. I don't know how long I'll be. I hope that I'll be back in time to get breakfast going."

Mama Nettie slipped into some clothes, and left the bedroom. She went out to the back porch, and slipped her feet into some black rubber boots and a black rain slicker. It was over a mile walk to the Smith's house, and she walked as fast as she could against the beating rain. When she reached the house, everything was calm. The young lady was lying quietly on a big bed, and the two younger sisters who had come out to call her were both standing next to the bed.

"What's going on?" Mama Nettie asked. "Where is the baby?"

One of the sisters pointed to a metal bucket, which sat in a dark corner of the dimly lit room. Mama Nettie walked over to the bucket and bent down to get a close look. There was a tiny corpse left in the bucket that looked like an old garfish that Art and I had pulled out of the river. They had not even attempted to wrap a blanket around the baby.

"When was the baby born?" Mama Nettie asked.

"Just a few minutes ago," replied one of the sisters.

"Can you just write on your report to Dr. Shipp that you delivered the baby?"

"What? You want me to falsify records? I'm afraid that I will have to report the truth, and the truth is that this poor baby was dead when I got here. I'll be happy to check your sister, but I'm afraid that is about all I can do here."

Mama Nettie walked over to the bed, and pulled the sheet away from the mother. She massaged her stomach and asked a few questions about the delivery. After inserting some packing cloth into the patient's uterus, she gave instructions for her care, and told the family that the doctor would be calling in a couple of days.

Sky Pines

Dad's recovery from his leg injury was limited. He still had the open wound, which had to be cleaned and bandaged twice every day. I can still remember that sickening odor that came from that leg at times. His pain was constant, so his ability to work was very limited, too. He did take a job as the gardener for the Sky Pines Estate, located on the Gin Road. This road was the famous site where the Favre family had constructed the cotton gin on the river.

Prior to 1880, there was a cemetery located on Gin Road about a half mile up on the right. My great-great grandmother, Harriet Garden Maxson, was buried there. Decades later when the cotton business faded along the Pearl River, Gin Road became a haven for a handful of very wealthy folks who built large homes along the river. Most of them lived in New Orleans during the week, and they used the homes for weekends and vacation retreats.

As the population of Gin Road continued to grow, Mama Adelaide feared that the cemetery and surrounding land would be plowed under eventually. So, one fall day around 1923, she marched up Gin Road with her wooden wheelbarrow and a shovel. There, she single-handedly dug her mother's bones up from her grave. Mama Nettie was obviously there too, because she told me that her grandmother's long hair had continued to grow after her death, and it had made a woven pattern around her bones and throughout the grave.

I don't remember hearing what Mama Adelaide did with her mother's remains, and I never saw any signs of a grave in the family plot at Pearlington Cemetery. Uncle Gene told me that when he was a very small boy, he followed his grandmother, Adelaide to a site in the woods. He hid behind a tree and watched as she danced and moaned around an earthen hill. Unfortunately, he couldn't remember the location of the mound.

I said earlier that Dad was the gardener at the Sky Pines Estate, but I should have said that Dad was the foreman, and Art and I did most of the gardening. Before we started school, we worked there year-round, but afterwards, our work was limited to time off on holidays and summer vacations.

Our job was to clear the grounds by raking and hauling the tons of pine needles, cones, and downed limbs. We would make large piles and once we were done, it was Dad's job to set the fires and supervise the burning. Dad did the grass cutting and worked on the mowers to keep them running, but reading his Bible seemed to take up most of his time. When Art was big enough to push the mowers, he helped Dad to cut the grass, too. I was never allowed to touch the lawn mowers because I didn't weigh enough to control them, and whenever I did beg Art to let me have a try at it, I was dragged and flapped about by the great, self-propelled machines.

The large estate called Sky Pines belonged to Mr. Hansel and his wife. He owned a big office supply store in New Orleans. Mr. and Mrs. Hansel had no children, and they seldom came out to the country, but when they did, they would call Dean's General Store to leave a message. On the day before their arrival, Mama Nettie and I would go into the house to sweep up and dust the furniture.

The house was a log cabin with a little side porch. At lunchtime, we would retreat to the porch to eat our sandwiches and drink cool water. Afterwards, we would lie on the floor for a nap while the afternoon thunder rumbled through the tall pines.

Summer days were always hot and muggy, and the refreshing afternoon rains from the daily thunderstorms always smothered the sweltering heat of noonday. Back in those days, we didn't have electricity to power fans, and air conditioning was still a distant dream. Those welcome storms cooled the unbearable heat, and cleaned some of the humidity from the air.

The hurricane season runs from June through November, and whenever tropical storms or hurricane force winds came through, they left behind a tangled mess of limbs and leaves. Sometimes, the tops of many of the yellow pines were snapped off like wooden matches. The Pearl River and surrounding bayous would flood, and leave a mess of swamp grass and twigs on the lawns and roads. We loved the stormy season, and we would go out to wade in the floodwaters. Only God saved us from the snakes, gators and leeches.

There was a big garage out behind the house, and it was made of logs, too. The garage had a large room attached to it. The room contained a single bed, a desk with a straight-back, wooden chair, and a big comfortable armchair and ottoman. A small bathroom with a shower was just off the room. The lawn mowers, carts and garden tools were kept in the garage. The tools hung neatly on the wall, and the machines were set in a straight line along the wall on the white gravel floor.

I was always afraid to enter that garage because of my fear of snakes. Dad and Art had found a few fat water moccasins when the snakes had retreated to the cool shelter of the garage. Whenever Dad sent me to fetch a rake or some tool, I was literally struck with terror, and I ran the errand as fast as my skinny legs would carry me.

We didn't mind the work. It seemed like a game to us, and there was always lots of time for fun as we scampered about filling and running with the two-wheeled carts. The grounds were so massive that it took a week to clear the entire yard. We soon learned the pattern, and every day we cleaned another section. We always got an early start to beat the summer heat of mid-day, and the early afternoon thundershowers. When the sun came out, Dad started the fires, and we waited until they had burned out before we could leave for the day.

The most fascinating thing at the Hansel estate was the presence of two alphabet trees. The trees stood in the front yard near the road, and they were covered with every letter of the alphabet as far up as I could see. I remember standing in front of those amazing trees and tracing my finger over every letter.

One day, Mr. Hansel took me out to the front yard and showed me those trees.

"How did these letters get here?" I asked.

"Why, they just grew here because these are real alphabet trees," Mr. Hansel replied.

I believed him, and I'm still in denial that no such tree exists. When Art told me that the letters had been carved in when the trees were young saplings, the truth struck me like a dull sword. I still prefer to continue believing Mr. Hansel's explanation. Some things should just be left to fantasy.

Mr. Hansel was probably one of the wealthiest men in New Orleans, and he sent a check to my grandfather every month for $14. Seventy cents per day doesn't seem like much now, but back in 1952, my grandparents depended on that monthly check to pay for the newly installed electricity, the tab at Dean's Grocery Store and other household expenses. When old man Tommy Dean died, his daughter, Ernestine, and her husband, Red Davis, took over the operation of the store. Everyone called Ernestine "Sister Dean," and when we were kids we called her "Miss Sister Dean."

Dad managed our little farm and did what he could around the house. When he was about 50 years old, he had a heart attack. He still did the same amount of work around the house, but he no longer smoked those short Lucky Strike cigarettes.

The near bout with death must have helped Dad to find his calling because by the time he turned 55 years old, he was ordained a Methodist Minister. Years later, he would become the pastor of Mama Nettie's beloved Holmes Chapel United Methodist Church. I guess all of that Bible studying at Mr. Hansel's estate had finally paid off.

Dad was quiet around the house most of the time. He read from his Bible and wrote the sermons that he delivered every Sunday. He was always humming some

Spiritual, and the sound of those tunes filled the house with a securing serenity.

When I heard that old man Hansel had passed, I felt confident that he would leave the estate to us, and I was overwhelmed when I learned that he had not. We had spent the greater part of our childhood cleaning the grounds and caring for the little log cabin. Somehow, it felt like a second home to me too, and it was as though I had lost an old friend when the property went to Mrs. Hansel's distant niece.

Miss Fryeburg

Miss Fryeburg was a short, round, little lady who owned a store around the corner from the house on Highway 604. She was new to the Pearlington community. By the time I started second grade in Logtown, Miss Fryeburg purchased the only other store in town from Mr. John Bayer. I would never forgive Miss Fryeburg for telling Mr. Reinhardt where we lived on that black day at the great sawdust piles.

Miss Fryeburg had a little of everything, from sewing needles to long rolls of sandwich meat. Before the installation of electric lights and butane gas, Art and I were sent to her store to buy kerosene for the heaters and oil lanterns; or to get five slices of liver cheese. We pulled our little wagon, and she would fill the oil tanks and put them back in the wagon for us.

It was here at Miss Fryeburg's that I got to pick out whatever flour sack struck my fancy. The flour was packed in beautiful cotton sacks. There were flower patterns in soft pastel colors of pinks, blues, and yellows. The sacks stood on the floor propped against the counter on the left side of the store. When I had a dress in every pattern, I would worry Miss Fryeburg every day until the new shipment of flour sacks came. Mama Nettie would wash, starch and iron the cotton cloth before cutting out the patterns to make my dresses.

The little store was dark and drab. The counters ran down both sides and across the back of the store, and the center isles were filled without much consideration to order. There were two entrance doors in the front, and doors on either side that were made of heavy boards. The store showed no signs of paint on the outside or the inside, and the old rain-washed boards seemed as old as the town itself.

A glass display case ran along the left side of the store. It was filled with sewing needles, colorful spools of thread, knitting needles and yarn, embroidery hoops, cloth, threads, and needlepoint supplies. The cotton flower sacks sat on the floor and were leaning against the glass case in a random fashion. There was a row of wooden shelves behind the counter that held household items like flower vases, mason jars, candles and kerosene lanterns. There were two, five-foot long shelves in the center of the store. These shelves held canned goods like: sardines, beets, creamed corn, and evaporated milk.

Wooden shelves ran from the floor to the ceiling on the right side of the store, and these shelves held pots, pans, nails and hardware items. A large counter ran across the back of the store, and there was a glass display case that held cold cuts and cheeses. A large meat cutter sat on the countertop next to a scale, and Miss. Fryeburg would place a piece of white, butchers paper on the scale, and stack the slices of meat until she reached the desired weight. Crates of Irish potatoes, onions, apples, oranges, and bananas were placed around the store, and there were great burlap sacks of rice and dried beans. There was a pump behind the back counter for the kerosene that we purchased for the oil lanterns and stoves.

When Miss Fryeburg didn't have a customer in the store, she could be found sitting in a rocking chair near the side door of her store. She was always reading, and her tiny, rimmed glasses sat perched on the tip of her short, pink nose. She had bright blue eyes and shoulder-length grayish-blonde hair. Miss Fryeburg didn't own a car, and she made the short walk from her house near the river to the store each morning.

Miss Fryeburg didn't have a family, or should I say she did not have a human family, for her children were three fat Labradors. The dogs looked like their owner. They were all thick with the same color of grayish-blonde hair. The dogs, Frieda, Max and Greta, ran about happily as they walked to and from the store, and they always sat on the floor at Miss Fryeburg's feet as she read or nodded in the afternoon sun. If Miss Fryeburg went behind the counter, the dogs followed her there. Though we didn't seem to mind, the store was always filled with the unmistakable odor of the three hounds. Sometimes I think about her, and I wonder if she ever washed her hands before she went behind the counter to slice those cold meats that we loved so well.

Our First Job

Ernie was eight, I was seven and Art was six years old when we got our first job. Of course, Art and I had farmed for Dad for at least four years, but there were no remunerations there. Miss Fryeburg hired "The Three Pioneers" to wash her dishes and sweep up her house. Our rate of pay was set at 50 cents per day. We were excited about earning our first wages.

We showed up on time at 6:30 a.m. so she could show us around the mansion before she left to open her store. As soon as we stepped into the house, we were smacked in the face by an odor that must have been ten times worse than the one at the store. Here in the house, it smelled like Frieda, Max, and Greta had once had seven more sisters and brothers, and from the odor, they had all died and were buried in the living room.

The kitchen had a cold water tap, and every dish in Pearlington must have been piled up in and around the sink. There was a dishpan filled with cold, smelly water, and there was a scum floating on top of the dishwater that looked like the boiled cream in Dad's steaming coffee.

Mama Nettie had already taught us the importance of keeping one's word, and we knew that there was no way to back out of this deal so we dove in and worked for about five hours. There's no way to say that we left the place bright and shiny, but we did the best that we could.

When we got home, Mama Nettie put the big kettles of water on the stove for us to take a bath, and we told her about our experience while the water heated. We must have smelled pretty bad, because she threw in a handful of her lavender bath salts when the bath was ready.

"Now you get washed up while I fix your lunch."

We each took our bath and changed into clean clothes. Mama Nettie had our lunch ready and waiting for us when we were done. After we had eaten, she looked around the table at each of us and said, "I'm mighty proud of you children for going out and finding work on your own, but I think I will talk to Dad tonight to see if he can start paying you all a weekly allowance. That way, you won't have to go out to work for someone else." We were elated. No one wanted to go through that experience again.

The next day, Dad told us that we would each get two bits a week. That was the term used for 25 cents back then. Twenty-five cents would buy two Nehi Sodas, a Stage Plank Gingerbread Cookie with pink frosting, two Long Boy Candy Sticks, miscellaneous wads of Double Bubble Chewing Gum, and we'd still have enough left over to put a nickel in the church plate on Sunday. We were rich!

Chapter XI

Big Changes

Leaving the Farm

Art and I didn't know it then, but as summer drew to an end so would our simple, happy lives on the farm with Mama Nettie and Dad.

One day, Mama Nettie called the two of us in for a talk. She sat in her armless rocking chair where she had held us and prayed so many times before. Today, she pulled us close to her, and I wondered if someone was sick or had died. I held my breath to hold back the fear.

"I have something to tell you," she said. "Your Mama has gotten married, and she wants to take you children home with her so that you all can be a family. You know how much Dad and I love you, and I hate to see you go, but your place is with your mother."

We stared at Mama Nettie with mixed confusion. I was elated to be with my beautiful mother, yet heartbroken as I watched the tears stream down Mama Nettie's face. We began to cry too as she gently hugged us to her chest. I will never forget those loving arms or the comfort of my head snuggled close to her.

A few days later, Mama pulled up to the house for us. We loaded our things into the trunk of the car, and she and my grandmother exchanged a few words. "You take care of my babies," Mama Nettie said, "and remember, you can always bring them back if things don't work out."

"It's time for us to go," Mama said.

Mama Nettie held out her arms, and she sat down on the front steps to give us both a big hug. We kissed her and ran to get into the car. As we pulled away, we could still see the tears glistening on her cheeks in the late afternoon sun.

Things did not work out well between my stepfather and us, and within six months, Art would be back with my grandparents. It would take seven years for me to make my way back, but in the interim, Mama Nettie was always there with open, loving arms. I would get to pass most weekends, summer vacations and holidays there on the little farm where I had learned so much about life in such a short time.

The Destroyer

When my mother's older sister, Myrtle, lived on Whites Road, her house sat about one hundred feet from a canal that connected Whites Bayou to the Pearl River. We called the canal The Branch. There was a cattle gap over the canal that was made of thick wooden beams, and it was designed to keep the cows from traveling the few short blocks to Highway 604. We never dared to cross the cattle gap after dark. At dusk, we would stand on the road above to watch giant, gray-black water moccasins as they did their evening dance in the shallow water below.

Aunt Myrt and Jim Bo had three children: Iris Cleo was the oldest; Alvin, whom everyone called Brother, was their only son; and Gay Carol was the baby.

The girls were gone most of the time because they stayed with Jim Bo's relatives in Slidell, where they attended school. Brother was only four years older than me, but he was more than double our size in both height and girth. We all tried to avoid him as much as possible because he always tormented us and destroyed everything that we had of value.

I recall one summer day in the early 1950s when a two-story, cinder block building went up on the lot next to Mama Nettie and Dad's house to replace the old wooden structure. There was a large, empty room on the first floor that was used as a hall and meeting place for the black folks in the community. The second floor held the secret chambers of the Masonic Order of Odd Fellows, and the Order of The Household of Ruth.

The door to the secret chambers was always locked. Dad was a member of the lodge, so we always knew when something was going down because he would dress up like a retired war hero with banners and badges before leaving the house. Sometimes, on Friday nights when the Odd Fellows were holding one of their secret inauguration ceremonies, "The Three Pioneers" would climb the stairs and press our ears to the door. We never could hear any-thing more than muffled sounds coming from the quarters, so we would giggle, and tiptoe down the stairs to make our escape.

That same year, Mama Nettie rented a corner on the first floor of the Mason's Odd Fellows Hall and started a restaurant. A long counter curved around one corner of the large room. There was a stove and a sink behind the counter, and a few tables and chairs ran along the windows facing the street.

It was late summer, because I remember that Art and I had picked a ton of butter beans that year. I can still remember how sore my little fingers were after repeatedly poking my thumbnails under the tight rim of the bean pods as we sat on the floor of the restaurant.

We shelled beans for days, and one afternoon Brother stopped by the restaurant to pay us a visit. Mama Nettie gave all of us a slice of pie and a scoop of vanilla ice cream. While we were eating our snack, Brother said, "I see that you both have new canvas shoes."

"Yes, our Mama just bought them for us yesterday," I said proudly, and we each held up our new, white shoes for him to admire.

"I bet you don't know that those shoes make terrific sliders," he said. "You sure could have lots of fun with those shoes. I know just the game for you."

"How do you play the game?" I asked.

"Well, we can go outside, and I'll show you."

"Mama Nettie, can we go out to play now," I asked.

"Okay, but don't go any farther than the yard," she said.

There was a brick walkway from the front gate to the steps of the house. A red clay path led from the walkway, down the side of the house to the gate of the chicken yard. Brother took us there to the path.

"Okay, now here's what we have to do before the game can start. You two have to help me carry buckets of water to the path. We need to get it nice and slippery."

"Okay!" we shouted, and off we ran to retrieve buckets of water from the pump behind the house. We started at the brick walkway and poured water about 15 feet along the path.

"Is it ready yet?" Art asked.

"No, it has to be real soupy. We need a little more water."

We continued to struggle with the heavy buckets while the brute sat on the side steps, chewing on a piece of grass with a sinister grin on his lips.

"Alright," he yelled. "It looks just right now. You two go all the way back to the walkway and get a running start. When you get to the mud, throw on the brakes and let those mud skaters slide you down the path.

"But won't we get our shoes dirty?" I asked.

"Oh, don't worry about that, it will wash right off.

We started the game, and Brother continued to add water to the path as we rushed back and forth to slide through the orangey-brown goop. He was right. It was fun, and sure enough our new shoes made the best mud sliders ever. We let out screams of laughter as we slid and fell. We slipped down a few times, and before long we were both covered with mud from head to toe.

Soon, Mama Nettie came out to investigate the source of the commotion, and our fun was cut short. "What in heaven's name are you children doing?" she asked.

Art and I stood speechless, and I couldn't figure out what we had done wrong, but from the look on my grandmother's face, there was something about mud skating that was not quite pleasing to her.

"Look at you. You've ruined your new shoes, and you're both covered with mud," Mama Nettie said.

I tried to explain how Brother had told us to wet the path, and how he had said that the mud would wash right off our shoes, but Brother was no place in sight. He probably saw our grandmother coming, and he had run off and left us holding the bag. We got our hides tanned that day, but the thing that hurt the most was the fact that Brother, without a doubt, was someplace laughing his heart out at us.

The mud-slider trick was not the only joke that the bully played on Art and me. We got our first two-wheel bikes that Christmas. They were both red with solid rubber tires and training wheels. Art and I raced up and down the lane all that Christmas day, and when Brother came over to visit, we proudly displayed our new prized possessions. We parked the bikes under the covered patio off the back porch that night, but the next morning when we went out to ride our bikes again, they were missing. We returned to the house crying,

"Someone stole our bikes."

Mama Nettie and Dad came out to the yard with us, and eventually Dad found the bikes behind his old shed in the chicken yard. Someone had used an ax from the shed to chop off big chunks of rubber from the front tires of our new bikes. The old folks looked at each other with knowing glances. We didn't care what condition they were in. We took our bikes out to the lane, and bump-de-bump we happily went up and down the road in front of the old house.

Dad left out the back gate and went down Whites Road. A few minutes later he was back, and we saw him holding Brother by the collar.

"Do you see what you did to those bikes? Dog bite the luck. What in tarnation could make someone so spiteful and mean?" Dad gave Brother a hard swat on the ear with his gnarled hand. "Now you get out of my sight," Dad said. Brother turned and ran down the road toward his house.

On another occasion, Art and I were alone, and we were playing out in the front yard. Our nemesis came over and picked Art up.

"Go ahead, hook your legs on the limbs of the cedar tree before I drop you," he said. As soon as Art wrapped the back of his knees around the limbs Brother let go, and left him hanging upside down in the tree.

"Help," Art pleaded. Instead of taking him down Brother laughed, turned and ran off.

I stood helpless at the base of the tree. I was too short to reach him, but I could tell by the bright, red color of his ears that he needed to come down from that tree. Art hung there crying as the blood rushed to his head. Luckily, my grandparents were back within a few more minutes, and Dad rescued my brother from yet another cruel act at the hands of our family bully.

Time didn't improve Brother's disposition, and he grew into a menacing and abusive teenager.

Art continued to work the farm, and when he was old enough, Dad assigned the cows to him, too. The old house was located in the heart of town, and there was no place to pasture the cows on the little farm because Dad utilized every square inch for planting. Art was tasked with taking them to the woods every morning after they were milked, and he had to find them and herd them home before dark.

Jim Bo introduced Art to the forest, and he was soon strong enough to toss the giant logs across the bed of the long, pulpwood truck. Art played football in high school, and he had developed an ample supply of muscles by the time he turned fifteen.

One day the bully played his final trump card. Art was walking on the path between the Odd Fellows Hall and the side fence of the old house. Without warning, Brother stepped from behind the building and slammed a fresh cow pie into Art's face. Art didn't see it coming, and he stood stunned for a moment.

Brother was bent over with laughter as Art cleaned his face, and he didn't see it coming when Art bent down and ripped a board from the old outhouse. The board came off easily, but a rusty nail was still stuck in its base. Art turned with the swiftness of a ninja and hit the bully across the back. Brother's knees buckled, and he fell, face down to the ground. The rusty nail ripped through his flesh as Art pulled back and came down on him once again. This time, he caught Brother in the buttocks. Art raised the board once again, and he held it high over his head to deliver a third blow. At that point, Dad appeared out of nowhere and grabbed Art's arm.

"Stop, you're going to kill him," Dad said. Art loosened his grip on the board as he turned his head to look into Dad's eyes.

"That's exactly what I'm trying to do," Art replied.

"Now you know that Mama and I have raised you better than that," Dad replied. Slowly, Art removed his hand from the board, and the anger drained from his body.

Brother had already made his escape, but from that day on the bully had met his match, and he never dared to bother Art again.

I never could understand how my two cousins, Iris and Carol, could have been related to our tormentor, because they were so sweet and so opposite from their brother. The girls and I became best friends, and we were more like sisters than cousins.

Now for folks who don't know what cow pies are, they're the droppings of the great beasts. The big pie-shaped mess comes out sort of gooey, and splashes when it hits the ground. When the manure sets up for a while, it starts to get firm, and within a day or two it dries out completely. Since the cow's principal diet was composed of hay and grass, the old folks burned dried cow pies to repel mosquitoes. That's what we used long before S. C. Johnson came out with those little green, repellent coils.

Brother joined the Marines and did a tour in Vietnam. After his discharge from the service, he returned to Pearlington. He married three times, and each marriage ended in divorce. However, he did have six wonderful children who loved him despite his shortcomings. He loved his children too, and he took time to teach them right from wrong. He taught his son to walk in honor, and most of all, he taught them all to have faith and trust in God.

My grandmother always said that no matter how far we strayed, we would always be compelled to return our origin. "The apple cannot fall far from the tree," she always said. So even though Brother made many bad choices in life, he knew when it was time to return to his roots.

Thank goodness, with age comes wisdom. We all grew taller and wiser, and we learned to put aside our childhood gripes. The family was the most important thing to us and Brother was part of our heritage.

About a month before his 60th birthday, he suffered a massive coronary attack and slipped into a coma. The doctors summoned his family to advise that he was in a vegetative state with absolutely no brain functions. Art stood facing Brother's bed as the doctor concluded his briefing. Just then, Art stared at Brother in amazement.

The comatose patient lifted his hands and gave Art the thumbs-up sign. He could not speak, but tears welled up in his eyes as everyone gathered around. Brother squeezed Art's fingers and placed his closed fist to his heart in a gesture to let Art know that he loved him, and that everything was all right.

Later, he slipped back into a coma, and the family decided to remove the life support. To the doctor's astonishment, he continued to breathe on his own for more than a week before his life ended.

His sister, Carol and her husband, his children, and my brother, Art all kept vigil at his bedside before he died on July 11, 2005.

The Pie Shop

Mama Nettie ran the little restaurant in the Odd Fellows Hall for a year or two until she acquired a piece of land on the border of Pearlington and Logtown. The land had once belonged to her mother, and when she heard that it was being auctioned at the County Courthouse in Bay St. Louis, she went down to bid on it.

On the day of the auction, she stood near the steps of the courthouse with its tall, white columns and placed the first bid. She heard a man's voice coming over the crowd as he placed a higher bid. The two of them went back and forth, one bidding higher than the other. Finally, the man inched his way over to my grandmother and said. "Tell me, why do you want that property?"

Mama Nettie replied, "That land once belonged to my family, and I would like to get it back."

"Who are your people?" the stranger asked.

"My grandfather was Etienne Maxson, and his father was a Favre. That land was passed down to my mother," my grandmother replied. "Who are you, and why do you want the land?" Mama Nettie asked the stranger.

"I'm your cousin; my mother was your granddaddy's sister. You can have that land," he replied. "I just wanted to keep it in the family." He patted Mama Nettie's hand,

255

and walked away. She placed the final bid, and the land was hers. Once again, God had given her a miracle.

"Thank you, Jesus," Mama Nettie whispered as she counted out the last dollar to the court clerk.

Years later when Mama Nettie told me how she had reacquired the family land, she gave me some history about the kind kinsman that she'd met on the courthouse steps on auction day. I'm certain that she gave me his name, but all that I remember is that he was a member of the Bourgeois family. She did tell me that her distant cousin's father worked as a game warden, and one day while his parents were out on a boat ride, tragedy struck. His father placed his rifle across his legs and as he moved the oars through the water, the gun accidentally discharged and killed his mother.

The land was covered with oaks and pines. Mama Nettie's younger half-brother, nicknamed Baby Zeek, had learned the carpentry trade from his father, Pappy Zeek, and he was famous for his log cabin constructions. He had built Mr. Hansel's log home in The Gin, and one for himself, too. Mama Nettie had decided to build her own restaurant, and she asked her brother to build a log cabin for her.

"I want it to be more than a place to eat. I want to have a nice place for young people to come to have good, clean fun."

Dad, Uncle Gene and Uncle Jim Bo all came to help. Jim Bo cut down the pine trees, and the men worked together to skin the logs. Within a few months the work was done. The little, two-roomed log cabin sat near the road on Highway 604, about five miles up the highway from Whites Road. Mama Nettie planted azalea bushes across the front of the cabin, and a wire fence enfolded the rest of the property. A big Coca Cola sign stood out front and proudly displayed the name, "Arnette's Pie Shop."

Mama Nettie had two glass showcases at the back of the restaurant, placed in an "L" shape. There was a rect-angular, chest-type soda machine, which sat on the floor to the far left of the room, and metal racks held the bot-tles by the neck as they floated in ice-cold water. There were six or seven tables scattered about the large room, and each table was covered with red and white, checkered tablecloths. Mama Nettie sewed bright curtains on her old Singer machine, and fresh cut flowers were placed around the room.

The back room housed the kitchen with a stove, a refrigerator, some counter tops and a sink. A big table sat in the middle of the room. There was a six-foot high wall between the kitchen and a little area about eight feet wide, which held a bed and a small table.

That first summer, and a few summers after that, I went out to Pearlington to help in the restaurant. Ernie, Art and I kept the soda machine stocked. We stacked the tables and chairs together to sweep and mop the restaurant, and we washed dishes and kept the kitchen clean. We always had a good time together and no matter what the job was, we found a way to sneak in a little fun.

One day, we were scrubbing the linoleum floor in the kitchen. We always used too much of everything we touched, and a little extra Tide Detergent and Pine Oil surely wouldn't hurt. We had a nice slippery suds going, and we decided to have a skating match. Ernie took a long skid and hit the deck. When she fell, the oven door flew open. She attempted to close the door, but she continued to slip and was not able to get up. Art and I rushed over to help her up, and the two of us slipped and fell in the suds too. "The Three Pioneers" struggled there on the floor, each clawing at the other and laughing until our sides hurt.

The showcases were filled with Mama Nettie's cakes and pies. Soon, word spread as far away as New Orleans. The pastries were probably a bigger success than the restaurant, and soon after opening, she was forced to have a telephone installed. Clients called to order the cakes and her special sweet potato, lemon meringue, and apple pies.

When it was time to close down for the night, sometimes we were all too tired to make the five-mile journey to the old house. Mama Nettie and Dad would retire to the little bed off the kitchen, and Ernie, Art and I would pull a few tables behind the glass showcase, and soften them up with quilts to make our bed for the night.

A jukebox sat just inside the doorway to the right, and true to her word, every Friday night my grandmother had a dance for the kids. Most of the kids were teenagers, but there were a lot of little squirts like us, too. We danced, laughed, and had a great time.

Mama Nettie drew a big circle on the floor with chalk and added boxes that she numbered for the cake walk game. Everyone would stand on a number. When the music began, we would march around the circle. When the music stopped, someone would pull a number from a box, and the prize went to the person standing on the winning number. Everyone loved Mama Nettie's cakes, so the cakewalk was the most popular game.

The restaurant was always filled at lunchtime, and we knew that many of the visitors were not paying customers. Mama Nettie never lost her vision. She always strove to treat everyone with dignity and respect, and that meant that no hungry man, woman, or child would ever leave her place with an empty stomach.

In 1960, the imminent arrival of the National Aeronautic and Space Administration struck joy into the hearts of most of the inhabitants of Pearlington, Logtown, Gainesville, and Napoleon, when it was thought that the agency would bring prosperity back to the area. However, NASA snapped up miles of land to create a buffer zone around the rocket testing facility. Of the four towns, only Pearlington was spared. The other three towns were demolished. Every brick and board was leveled, and the only things left were a few cement slabs and the giant azalea bushes that had once adorned beautiful gardens.

The Pie Shop property sat right on the border of the buffer zone, so Mama Nettie made plans to build a motel to provide temporary housing for some of the incoming workers.

Government Inspectors

The Pie Shop had been up and running for about two years when two young men, Tony and Johnny, moved from New Orleans to Pearlington. They bought a piece of land about a quarter of a mile from the pie shop and built a metal house on stilts. When the house was completed, they started raising chickens. One day, they came down to talk to Dad. They were looking for someone to clean the birds, and they asked if he would be interested. Dad told them yes because they were paying twenty-five cents per chicken.

Art and I were just getting the hang of things, and we realized that Dad was great at delegating work out to us. Art and I were assigned with the chore of cleaning, gutting, and inspecting two or three crates of smelly chickens every Saturday morning. I don't believe that anyone who ever took on the gruesome task of chopping off a chicken's head, and dipping the quivering beast in boiling water could ever forget that smell. Needless to say, years went by before I could stand to eat a morsel of chicken again.

Dad got us all set up behind the pie shop. There was a pump with a big tub of cold water underneath, and a black, cast iron pot sat steaming near a white enameled counter top. Dad taught us how to hold on to the chicken's feet while we submerged the whole bird in the boiling water. We then moved them to the counter where we plucked the feathers. After a dip in the cold water, we cut their bellies open and removed the internal mess. We cleaned the gravel and gunk from the gizzards, and took great care not to let the bile duct rupture onto the liver. The liver, gizzard, heart and neck were placed back into the freshly washed bellies, and a bright purple sign, "U.S.D.A. Inspected," was stamped on the thick, white breast of the birds.

Dad always had a few hunting dogs around, and he moved them between the house and the Pie Shop. Bullet was his favorite pet, and he had to be about the ugliest dog that I had ever seen. He was rather medium-sized with salt and pepper hair. His tail was too long to be bobbed, and too short to be a tail. It looked as if he'd tangled with a bobcat, and the bobcat had won, for the tip of his right ear had been chewed off. Something had happened to one of his hind legs, and he hopped about like a rabbit.

Dad always cooked cornmeal mush, and mixed it in with table scraps to give his dogs a hearty meal. He gave Bullet more than the other dogs, and I often wondered why he loved that ugly dog so much. Years later, Art told me that Bullet was, in fact, a hero. He had saved Dad from the attack of some beast in the woods.

One Saturday morning, Art and I were out back working feverishly to clean the two crates of chickens that had come in from the chicken farm that morning. Our fire was going, and we were making good progress when we heard a horn blowing in the driveway along the right side of the Pie Shop. I peeped around and saw that it was Mama, and we both ran out to greet her. We lost track of time, but it couldn't have been more than five minutes when we remembered the chickens.

We both ran back to the work site and sure enough, that ugly mutt Bullet and his pals had carted off at least ten chickens. There were twenty-five chickens to a crate, and ten was ten too many to lose. We retrieved a few from the yard and continued to search. There was a peanut patch about fifty yards to the left of us, and we went there to look for the birds, too. Sure enough, we found most of them buried under the straw in the peanut patch. That Bullet was a sneaky critter too.

We washed the purloined chickens for hours trying to get the dirt, dried grass, and twigs unglued from the exposed flesh. A couple of those birds were too mangled to salvage so we just returned the cleaned chickens, and hoped that Tony and Johnny wouldn't notice the shortage. Although we knew that Dad had done the right thing, this time only, he let us slide by.

Chapter XII

Facing Life's Hardships

A New Family for Us

We moved to Bay St. Louis with Mama around the end of summer in 1954, and our sister, Faith, was born on Veterans Day that same year. Art and I started school in September at St. Rose de Lima Catholic School. The classes were so small that they combined second and third grade, so Art and I were in the same classroom.

Things were not easy for us. We were sheltered in the secluded, little community of Pearlington. The town folks there were like one big family. Here, things were different. We were strangers in a strange place. People stared and scrutinized us up and down, and I soon became shy and withdrawn. I often wondered if they hated us so much because we were different from other kids, or because we didn't have a real daddy.

The kids at the new school weren't friendly, either. It was amazing how second and third graders could be so cruel. I was called cat eyes, and mop head, and shunned on the playground. With Art they went one step further, and one day a group of boys lynched him with vines on the schoolyard.

My mother raised cane, and she stomped around town like Hitler tap dancing on the second floor. She reported the incident to the police and there was a trial. The kids were questioned, but nothing good came of it. The attitude of the kids worsened after that. Art was tormented continually, and I was just ignored.

Things did get better for me at school after a while. I had five good friends throughout high school: Chiquita Joseph, Melanie Robeteau, Joseph Tate, and Calvin and Marilyn Smith. All of my friends went on to have successful lives. Unfortunately, Joseph died in 2004 after a long illness.

Mama worked as a housekeeper for a wealthy family on the Beach Road. Every Thursday night, she stayed late to prepare for Mrs. Perry's bridge party, and it was on those nights that my stepfather, Ben, decided to push us extra hard to teach us proper penmanship or improve our mathematical skills.

"Make the swirls even. Can't you two get it right?" he said, and he would crack us across the back of our hands with a varnished yardstick. Before each Thursday evening was over, poor Art would be beaten within an inch of his little life, and I would usually end up with a taste of the strap too, because I cried and screamed for him to stop beating my brother.

My stepfather Ben's dad was a full-blooded Choctaw Indian, and his mother had Indian blood too. Ben had nine siblings. He wore a mustache and reminded me of a darker version of the popular cowboy, Paladin, on the TV show, *Have Gun Will Travel.* Ben drove a delivery truck for McDonald's Lumber Yard, and we lived in one of the company houses on State Street.

There were four or five little houses lined up in a row, and we stayed in the last one from the corner of Esterbrook Street. Each house had the same floor plan: a living room, kitchen, two bedrooms and an unfinished bathroom.

None of the interior walls were finished. The houses were thrown up with two-by-four frames, and wood siding was nailed to the exterior. In some places, you could see light through the cracks where the boards had shriveled under the hot summer sun. The house was freezing cold during the winter months, and I would hold my face to the wall to feel the cold air rushing through the open cracks on those cold winter mornings.

One freezing Thursday afternoon in February of 1955, Art and I were playing outside. It was nearly dusk dark.

"I can't take it anymore, Sis. I'm leaving here and going back to Mama Nettie and Dad's," he said. The tears rolled down Art's cheeks, and made his green eyes seem ever brighter.

"You're going to run away?" I asked. "No! Don't do it. He will kill you and me too, when they find you."

"You should come with me," replied Art.

"I want to, but I'm afraid, and besides, Mama needs me. They're always fighting. I have to stay to protect her."

With that, Art turned and walked away. I stood in the middle of the street, pleading with him to come back.

"Please don't leave me," I begged. I watched until he turned the corner, and I ran inside and sat on the couch and cried bitterly for my little brother. We had always been like two peas in a pod, and I don't ever remember being separated from him.

It was dark when Ben got home. "Where's your brother?" he asked as he walked through the doorway with my baby sister in his arms.

"He ran away," I replied.

"He did what?" Ben asked.

"He said that he was running away, and he left."

My stepfather gave the baby to me, and told me to take care of her while he went to pick my mother up from work.

Meanwhile, Art had walked about three miles to the highway, stuck his thumb out, and hitchhiked his way back to Pearlington. He was there only a few minutes when Ben and my mother pulled up. Mama Nettie walked to the front door of the Pie Shop, and Art stood behind her, clinging to the back of her dress.

"You two can just hold it right there," Mama Nettie said with a stern voice. "I let you take my children away from a good home because you wanted to have your family, but every since they left this house, they've been abused and mistreated. This little boy just hitchhiked 18 miles to Pearlington. He could have been killed. He told me that he wants to stay here with Dad and me, and by God you'll not be taking him away again. You can get the law to force me to give him up, but the next time he runs away, he may not be so lucky."

"Calm down, Mama," my mother said. "We only want what's best for the children. I won't take him away again. If he wants to stay, we won't force him to leave, and we never abused them. We only beat them when they needed it," my mother reiterated.

"Shirley, if I had beaten you every time you needed it, by God you'd be dead now. What about Gail?" my grandmother asked. "Does she want to come back too?"

"I don't know, neither of them ever said anything to me," Mama replied. "We'll bring her out on Sunday, and she can decide then."

I sat on the couch in the dark living room, still crying when my mother and stepfather returned home to tell me that they had found Art.

"He's safe. He made it to Pearlington, and he wants to stay with your grandparents, so he won't be living with us anymore. Do you want to leave too?" Mama asked me.

"I want to be with my brother, but I don't want to leave you, Mama," I replied.

I said my prayers, and reached under my pillow for the thick rubber band that I chewed on every night to put myself to sleep. I didn't know then that my decision that night would reroute my destiny, and send me on a long, winding path of pain and self-destruction. When I was older, I would blame myself for this poor decision, but as I matured, I realized that it was a decision that an eight-year-old child should never have been forced to make.

That Sunday, as Mama promised, she took me out to my grandparent's house, and Mama Nettie sat in her armless rocker and put me on her lap. I cried for a long time as she held me close to her, and when I stopped, we sat there in the silence until I was ready to talk.

"Do you want to come back to live with us?" Mama Nettie asked me.

"I want to be with you, but I want to be with Mama, too." And I began to cry again.

"You don't have to decide now, but if you ever want to come home, you know that Dad and I will always want you."

I convinced myself that somehow I could keep Mama safe if I stayed with her, so though I felt miserable the majority of the time, I decided to stay. Just before my 11th birthday, Mama purchased a house at 240 Washington Street in Bay St. Louis.

We were just two blocks from the beach, and the old Star Movie Theater was on the corner of Washington Street and the beach road. The little house was painted pink outside. It had a living room, dining room, and kitchen across the front, and a single bathroom divided the two bedrooms. The rooms were much larger than the McDonald house, but the biggest difference was that it was sealed tight with stucco glazed sheetrock on the interior walls. The windows were tight, and the dark, hardwood floors glistened.

I shared a bedroom with my sister, Faith. I loved the house, and since Mama was working hard to pay the $40 mortgage every month, I didn't mind waxing the floors, dusting and doing the household chores. My stepfather, Ben had served in the Army, and he taught me how to pull the sheets tight in order to make a proper bed. He would come in to inspect my work, and he bounced a quarter on the sheet to make sure that it was tight enough to pass military standards.

We had a television, so I got to see how other folks lived. I enjoyed rearranging the furniture and making the house look like a picture in a magazine. Though perfection was forced upon me, I began to enjoy the atmosphere of a clean, neat and tidy life. This would later turn into a mania, and as I grew older, I became compulsive.

When I turned 12, Mama and Ben added a large bedroom onto the back of the house for themselves, and they gave me their old room. For the first time in my life, I had a place of my own. I absolutely loved my room. I even built a little bookcase to hold my books and treasures. I had always shared a room with Art, Ernie, and then Faith, so this was a completely new experience for me.

Sara

Mama Nettie's phone number had become the first one on the board at the Hancock County Welfare Office in Bay St. Louis. They knew that she would never turn away a needy child, and she was always the one they called whenever they had a child no one else wanted.

One day, the Welfare worker called to tell my grandmother that there was a ten-year-old girl, named Sara Smith, in nearby Harrison County. The Harrison County authorities had found her abandoned and sleeping in a boxcar at the railroad yard. She had been abused too, and she had been run over by a car several years earlier and had suffered a severe head injury, which had damaged her eyes. Sara had already sustained 13 operations to correct her vision.

"We are trying everything we can think of to help Harrison County out, but there's no institution there or here in Hancock County that can take her right now. Please Arnette, can you help us?"

As usual, Mama Nettie had already made up her mind, but she never made any decisions without consulting Dad first. She always told me, "Dad and I are partners, and that means that we share the joys, the burdens, and the responsibility for everything that goes on in our house. We women must never forget that the man is always the head of the household, and it is up to the wife to give him that respect."

"I'll let you know something tomorrow," my grandmother replied. The next morning, she telephoned the Welfare Office and told them that they could bring Sara.

It was the summer of 1959. I was still living in Bay St. Louis with Mama, but as usual I spent the summer on the farm. Pappy died the year before, and Mama Nettie fixed up Pappy's old room for Sara.

On the day of Sara's arrival, "The Three Pioneers" oiled all of the furniture, and we helped Mama Nettie tidy up the old house. The three of us were standing inside the yard at the front gate when the car turned down our lane and stopped. No sooner had the car stopped than this strange being popped out from the back seat, like an electrified jack-in-the-box.

Sara was wearing a navy-blue, taffeta dress with pink piping. Her hair was shorter than a minute, and there was a large pink satin bow stuck in the top of her head with no visible means of support. She stood with her arms flapping about like a child pretending to fly, but the thing that frightened us the most was her eyes.

We knew that she had an eye injury, but no one had prepared us for the sight that we were now gazing upon. Sara wore thick glasses. The lenses were completely blacked out except for a tiny, round peephole that was about the size of a pencil eraser. We would eventually have a chance to see those eyes behind the scary glasses. The right eye was pointed northwest, and the left eye was aimed southeast. Mama Nettie told us that those tiny peepholes were designed to train Sara's eyes to look in the same direction. We really could never decide if she looked worse with her glasses on or off.

We stood there frozen and staring when out of nowhere, the other worldly being let out a loud, blood-curdling scream. She then turned and ran down the road like a bat out of hell. Sara was wing-footed, and as she ran she looked like a female version of Charlie Chaplain without the mustache.

"Hurry, run and get her!" Mama Nettie yelled to us. It was already too late. By the time we did hear her calling to us, we were already halfway through the chicken yard, and we ran as fast as we could through the fields and over the back fence. We didn't stop until we were tucked safely in the quiet seclusion of the dense woods.

We stayed in the woods as long as we could, and the three of us hoped that Mama Nettie would be just as frightened as we were and send that scary person back with the Welfare lady, if they could ever catch her.

"It's getting late," Ernie said. "We better go home."

To our dismay, and disappointment, Sara had been retrieved, and she now stood outside the door of her room. She made animal noises, and screamed as she did earlier. As we walked toward the kitchen, the fear left us, and anger kicked in. Sara was standing at the far end of the kitchen table. She held a heavy kitchen chair above her head like a lion trainer under the big tent, and she motioned it towards my grandmother.

"Hey," we all yelled in unison. "Put that chair down. We're not going to let you hurt Mama Nettie." Mama Nettie stood facing Sara with her back to us. Her eyes never left the enraged girl, and she raised her left arm to block us from entering the kitchen.

"Now you kids just leave me alone with Sara. I can handle this," Mama Nettie said.

"But she wants to hurt you," I said.

"I'll be alright," Grandmother replied. Reluctantly, we backed away.

Mama Nettie spoke to Sara with a calm, sweet voice. "Now you put down that chair. No one here is going to hurt you. You will never be hurt again." My grandmother continued to talk to Sara, and after several minutes, she sat the chair down and calmed down a little. Mama Nettie took her into her room and helped her to change clothes.

Over the next few years, Sara returned to the hospital three more times for eye surgeries. Her mental capacity was behind schedule, but the little, wild beast that emerged from the car that summer day developed into a happy, good-humored young lady. Mama Nettie taught Sara how to maintain personal hygiene, to cook, clean house and how to read and count. When Sara turned 15, she was declared legally blind, so the Welfare Department sent her off to a school for the blind in Northern Mississippi.

Mama Nettie called me into the kitchen one winter day. "I have some bad news for you," she said. "I was just notified by the Welfare Department folks that Sara was molested over a long period at the school, and she is already four months pregnant. They said that she's too far along for an abortion, so she will have the baby, and they will put it up for adoption."

"My Lord, How could they let that happen to her?" I asked. We both sat there crying like babies as we thought about the little girl who had come so far despite her past abuse and physical injuries. We wondered, too, if someone loving would be near to comfort her now.

Mama Nettie's sadness turned to anger, and she was down at the Welfare Office first thing Monday morning.

"Don't do this thing," she pleaded. "Let Sara come home. We can take care of her and her baby. I promised that little girl that her days of abuse were over when she came to live with us. She was doing just fine, and you took her off and didn't see to it that she was protected."

They were unshaken in their decision. "We will hold her until she delivers, and the baby will be placed for adoption." They did agree to return Sara to Mama Nettie's care when everything was over.

The officials did let Sara hold her baby girl for a moment, and she was allowed to name her little girl, Ruth, just before they cruelly snatched her away. When Sara came home, she was no longer an innocent, young girl who laughed loudly as we joked while I straightened her hair with a hot iron in Mama Nettie's kitchen. Sara was now a sad woman, but with Mama Nettie's wisdom and loving arms, she managed to regain some of the joy of her youth.

When Sara was a young adult, she met an older man from Pearlington, and he came to the house to ask Dad for her hand in marriage. They were married and raised a family. Sara was able to cook, clean house and care for her babies.

Gina

After LeNard, who was given to Mama Nettie just a few minutes after his birth, Gina was the second youngest child to go to my grandparents. The Welfare Department called Mama Nettie to ask for her assistance.

"We have a healthy baby, and there is no place for her. Can you help us, Mrs. Giles?" They explained that Gina's mother had been in prison, and she had been released to have her baby. After the birth, her mother was in a mall shoplifting. When the police started chasing her, she threw the baby through the open window of a parked car and continued her escape. The police caught her and she was returned to prison. However, the abandoned baby was left without a home. Gina was just nine days old.

Mama Nettie remembered the anguish that she and Dad had gone through with Kenny, and she told the Welfare folks that they would take the baby, but they wanted to adopt her. Mama Nettie was 56 years old by then, and she and Dad were already beyond the legal age to adopt children. It took quite a while before they were able to get around that stumbling block, but finally, Gina was theirs.

Mama Nettie was ill during this period and just a few weeks after taking Gina, she went to New Orleans for surgery to remove a tumor from her neck. After surgery, the doctors told her that the tumor was malignant, and they gave her six months to live.

"I want you to keep this information confidential. I don't want my family to know a thing," Mama Nettie said. That night as my grandmother lay in the hospital bed, she prayed and asked God, "Please Lord, all I ask is that you let me live long enough to raise this baby, and when my mission is complete, Thy will be done!"

Mama Nettie never told anyone about the cancer. She seemed to be back to normal within a few weeks, and carried on as usual. Around the fall of 1963, she became ill again after receiving a flu shot. She was hospitalized in Slidell Memorial Hospital. The diagnosis was mononucleosis. She was given a blood transfusion, and she remained in the hospital for about a month.

The strange illness persisted, and when she failed to respond to conventional treatments, the doctors began doing research on her. They tried a number of different experimental drugs from Europe and Japan. Most of the drugs had devastating side effects. One drug caused her to lose all of her hair. Another drug caused her shoulders to swell as if she were wearing a football player's shoulder pads. These first two conditions were reversed once the drugs were discontinued. Another drug caused her beautiful, creamy-tan skin to turn a blackish-gray tone, and it remained that way.

In the end, Mama Nettie was diagnosed with a rare form of "hypochromia anemia" that did not allow her to reproduce red blood cells. She was given frequent blood transfusions and stabilized on medications. No one ever really knew what was wrong with my grandmother, but as I reflect over her condition, I wouldn't be surprised if she had contracted AIDS from tainted blood transfusions.

Over the next 11 years, Mama Nettie would have several relapses. Though she was very ill, those 11 years were probably the most productive of her life.

Gina took piano lessons, and she was soon singing and playing music in Dad's churches. She developed into a beautiful young lady and helped Mama Nettie with the younger children. When she was old enough to drive, that became her second job, and she had fun chauffeuring Mama Nettie and Dad around.

Eighteen years earlier, Mama Nettie's wish had been to live long enough to raise that baby. The last earthly act that she performed before falling ill was to take Gina to Oral Roberts University to get her enrolled. After Mama Nettie's death, Gina and Kenny went to live with my Aunt Myrtle until she decided to go out on her own.

Chapter XIII

Laurels

Mrs. Baker and the School

Mama Nettie cleaned house for years for a Pearlington resident named Mrs. Irma Baker. Miss Irma, as we called her, had a big house with a white picket fence that sat about a block from the river. She had a little, chocolate brown Dachshund named Schotzy, and whenever she went out of town, Schotzy became a temporary member of our family, too.

Miss Irma was a little white lady with snow-white hair, and she taught at the School for Mentally Handicapped Children in Bay St. Louis. Miss Irma lived alone, and she and Mama Nettie spent most of the time talking whenever my grandmother went over to do housework. Art cut the grass, and Dad did odd repair jobs around her house, so I guess you could say that our family held the work monopoly at Miss Irma's place.

Mama Nettie also cleaned the Pearlington Methodist Church, which was located just across the street from Miss Irma's house. The church had an all-white congregation. It was beautiful inside, and it had a nice meeting room, a kitchen, rest rooms, and a handsome office for the pastor.

I went to help my grandmother out many times on Saturday afternoons just because I couldn't stand to see her so tired. Sometimes I would offer to go alone, but most of the time we worked together to get done. We would vacuum, dust the wooden pews and the altar, clean the bathrooms and wipe down the kitchen countertops.

Mama Nettie always said to me, "I'm praying that the Lord will make a way for us to renovate Holmes Chapel like this one day." As I indicated earlier, Mama Nettie always got the things that she prayed for.

Miss Irma knew all the details about the children who came to my grandparent's home. One Saturday afternoon, Mama Nettie went over to Miss Irma's as usual. She entered the kitchen and called out to her old friend, "Irma, its Nettie."

"Hello!" Miss Irma replied. "Come in here Nettie, I want to talk to you about something." Mama Nettie walked into the living room where she found Miss Irma sitting in her favorite chair. "Sit down Nettie." Mama Nettie sat on the couch, and Schotzy jumped up and put his head in her lap.

"You know, I've been thinking. We've been sitting here talking for years and it just hit me last night while I was lying in bed. I was thinking that there's not a more compassionate or talented person in the world. You've done remarkable things with those children that you've taken in. I just thought that you would be the perfect person to work with mentally retarded children at the school."

They sat there for a long time, and Mama Nettie didn't say a word. She stroked Schotzy's brown head, and after a few minutes she looked at Miss Irma and said, "I know that I've had good results with my children because I smother them with all the love that they've never had before. I believe that's why they respond so well to me. Children, no matter how retarded they are, can still recognize if someone's sincere with them or not. I have no formal education. I wouldn't know what to do."

"Now don't you go fretting, Nettie. What you have is far more valuable than any piece of paper that an educated person could produce. What you possess is a gift from God, and I tell you that you would be an asset to the school and a blessing to the children. Will you think about it?"

"Well, if you really think that I could help in some way, I'll just have to pray on it," Mama Nettie replied.

"All right then, why don't you just make us a cup of tea," Miss Irma said. "And while we're waiting for that water to boil, grab two glasses. Let's have a toast with some of that good brandy."

Mama Nettie went out to the kitchen with Schotzy following close on her heels. She returned to the living room with two small glasses. "Just pour a thimble full for me, Irma. You know I don't drink."

As Mama Nettie promised, she prayed on the matter, and that following Saturday afternoon, she gave Miss Irma her answer. She stood in the kitchen tying an apron around her waist.

"Well, I prayed on it as I promised, and the Lord wants me to do everything that I can to help His 'special children.' So, if you really think that I can do it, I will be glad to be of service."

Miss Irma rushed over to the sink where Mama Nettie stood and hugged her tightly. "Oh Nettie, you're going to do just great!"

The two women stood there in Miss Irma's kitchen, patting each other on the back, and they filled the big house with their laughter.

The official name of the school was the Hancock County Retarded Children's Association. It was governed by a board, and funded almost completely by the Hancock County United Fund. It was located in a school building in Bay St. Louis.

There were just a few children initially, but Mama Nettie knew of more children in Pearlington, Kiln, Delisle and other areas. She had cared for many of them in her home over the years. The only problem was that the school did not provide transportation for the children, and there was no way for the poor families to make the 18 to 25-mile journeys to the school and back home each day.

"No mountain is too high, and no ocean is too deep if you want to accomplish something," Mama Nettie always told me. "Just take it to the Lord in prayer."

My grandmother always practiced what she preached, so there was no stopping her. She filled up Dad's old car with every mentally challenged child that she could find. She often drove over eighty miles a day to pick up and drop off the children.

When a new public school was opened in Clermont Harbor, Mississippi, they were given one large room in a cinder block building. A decision was made to split the class into two sections. The "non-trainable section" was assigned to Mama Nettie. These were the children who were deemed unable to learn regular scholastic material. The Hancock United Fund continued their support for this section of the school. Miss Irma was assigned the "educable section" for the less handicapped children, and this section was funded under the regular Hancock County School System.

Mama Nettie recognized that every child is an individual. "The mentally handicapped child goes through different phases of ability. When they're in an off or non-receptive period, I leave them alone, but when they're in tune, that's when I push them. It's useless to force these children to do anything when they're not receiving the transmission. During that period, if I say 'Johnny, turn right,' he will invariably turn left.

"During the down time, I withdraw the training and concentrate on areas where they seem to have an individual expertise. The one thing that remains constant is my compassion and show of affection for the children. I never withdraw the love. Affection is the one area where they always seem to be open. Instead of yelling, they are more responsive to a hug. I maintain firmness and reprimand them, too, when they do something out of line, but it's delivered with a sound explanation as to why the act was inappropriate."

Mama Nettie always tried to teach all of us, as well as her handicapped children, that we should be proud of who we are. "It doesn't matter if you're the President of the United States or a ditch digger. Do your job to the best of your ability and always finish what you start." Those words echoed in my head long before "The Three Pioneers" took our first job at Miss Fryeburg's so many years ago. She wanted all of her children to have self-esteem, and she never let a day go by without trying to instill that into our heads.

"Be proud of yourself and make your family proud. Always think before you speak and think before you act. Don't ever do anything wrong to misrepresent your family."

Mama Nettie taught her school children how to take care of themselves by practicing daily, personal hygiene. If the families were too poor to purchase deodorant or toothpaste, she bought those things for them. She taught them how to do chores like cooking and cleaning house.

She went on to amaze the doctors and psychiatrists, who said that her children did not have the capacity to read or write. She kept files on each child and made notes on the periods when they were most receptive to learn, and she developed a system, and put it into practice. To the amazement of everyone, her children were learning to read, write, add, and count money. They were developing into functional people.

Mama Nettie continued her work at the school, and all the while she always had a houseful of children to care for at home. Every morning was a fiasco to get everyone up and going. They had long since abandoned the old house. They simply outgrew it.

Mama Nettie and Dad purchased two of the abandoned houses from the NASA buffer zone for a few hundred dollars each, and they paid several thousand dollars to have the wooden structures moved to Pearlington, set up on cement footings and connected to the utilities.

The larger of the two buildings that they purchased was placed on the lot directly behind the old house facing Whites Road. The sugarcane field was located there in days gone by. The movers also added three bedrooms down one side of the house, and they poured a cement slab across the front to add a porch.

The original house was composed of three large rooms and one bathroom. The first room was the living room, and the second room was a large kitchen. The third room was transformed to a dormitory for the six boys in the house.

The three new rooms gave Mama Nettie and Dad a bedroom to the front of the house off the living room. The older girls, Sara and Gina, shared another of the new bedrooms, and the younger girls shared the third one. The new "old house" now had four bedrooms, and still only one bathroom. Eventually, Dad and Uncle Gene added two more rooms across the back of the house. One was used as a study for Dad, and the other was used as a bedroom for Mama Adelaide and her fourth husband, Mr. Oscar White, when Mama Nettie took them in.

The smaller building was moved to the land up the road next to the Pie Shop. Work began to convert the house to a motel, and Mama Nettie planned the design and functionality of the building.

Work was well underway, and we were all excited about the prospect of being in the lodging business. Unfortunately, there were folks who didn't share our joy, and one, dark night in October 1960, the motel went up in flames. The town folks turned out to watch it burn. There was no fire department, and the wooden building was quickly consumed. The fire was an obvious case of arson, because neither gas nor electricity had yet been connected to the building.

Rumors spread that everyone from the Ku Klux Klan to irate neighbors were responsible. Somehow, Mama Nettie found out who the perpetrator was, and she made it her business to speak to the four young men: two blacks, and two whites, who had poured gasoline around the building and struck a match to ignite the flames.

"I know that it wasn't your idea, and I know who paid you to do such an evil deed. The good Lord knows that I've never done any harm to anyone. You all know that, to the contrary, I did everything I could to help when you were needy. We shared our food and loaned your papas money. I nursed your mothers back to health and made medicine for you when you fell ill. I've never asked for anything in return, and yet, this is how you repay me. The Lord will deal with you all, and I will pray for you, but as sure as I'm standing here today, you will all die with your boots on."

Mama Nettie's prediction struck fear into the hearts of many, and though she didn't lift a finger or even turn them in to the sheriff, one by one, they all met with tragic deaths. I often wondered if they were struck down by God's wrath for the mistreatment of my grandmother, or did they just die because she no longer interceded for their well being?

Every morning, Mama Nettie was up early to get the grits or oatmeal going. She put the coffee on for Dad, and started waking the kids up to take their turns in the single bathroom. Everyone had to take care of their toiletries, make their beds, get dressed and get to the breakfast table by 6:40 am. The older children helped the younger ones.

The dishes were stacked in the sink, and she was out the door by 7:00 am.

A couple of kids in the house piled into the car with her, and they were off to make the rounds in Pearlington to pick up three more children. Mama Nettie would drop off the first load of children at school, and head out to collect others from the Kiln and Delisle. (The town of Kiln, pronounced "Kill," has always been referred to as "The Kiln."

The Kiln has become famous in recent years because it is the home of the great NFL quarterback, Brett Favre. Brett is also a direct descendent of Simon Favre.

Most of the children attended regular classes at Charles B. Murphy Elementary School in Pearlington, or the high school in the Kiln, and they waited with Dad for the school bus to pass. Dad did not work outside the home, but he continued to preach. His schedule allowed him to be home during the weekdays, so he kept the younger children who did not attend school, and he did a few chores around the house. He washed up the breakfast dishes and would put on the infamous pot of beans for lunch.

By now, his hands were so gnarled that he could not do many things, especially when it came to picking up small objects. Their two-year old great-grandson, Jeremy, would button his shirt and tie his shoelaces. When it was time for

Dad to take his medicine, he would open the pill bottle and Jeremy would fish out a pill and place it in the sinkhole between Dad's thumb and his index finger. So, while Dad took care of the little ones, they took care of him, too.

Mama Nettie worked with her children at the school, and she kept pleading for more space and more equipment. "I think that it would benefit the children more if I could show them how to clean a real kitchen or make a real bed. We need a set-up with furniture and appliances for them to use. Maybe they can't learn to read books or go to college, but they can learn to live." Despite the lack of hands-on supplies, she did what she could to train the children to be self-sufficient and independent.

Eventually, businesses and individuals did donate furniture and appliances for Mama Nettie's project. Unfortunately, she was never allocated space to set up the rooms, so they shoved many of the items into a corner of the single classroom.

"It's a shame that we can't do this right, and have enough space to simulate a real house. The children are already agitated and confused. They need order in their lives," Mama Nettie said. Meanwhile, she continued to fine-tune her skills to make the children receptive to learning, and she never failed to shower them with love and affection.

Before long, some of her children were moved to the regular school system.

As the school population continued to grow, Mama Nettie asked for help. The funds were eventually appropriated, and she brought in my cousin, Iris Cleo Terrell-Hughes. Mama Nettie studied and passed her high school equivalency test at the age of 68.

That same year, Mama Nettie and Iris attended the Jefferson Davis Campus of the Mississippi Gulf Coast Community College in Gulfport, Mississippi to earn the required credentials to teach at the school.

President Richard M. Nixon presents the National Volunteer Award plaque to Mrs. Arnette Giles

Among friends and relatives in Washington for the presentation of the National Center for Voluntary Action Award received by Mrs. Arnette Giles were, standing l.to r., Mr. Perry Gibson, President, Hancock County Chamber of Commerce; Mrs. Frances Franckiewicz, Director, Hancock County Welfare Dept.; Mrs. Gwen Ishem, a life-long friend of the Giles'; Mrs. Mae Beyer, Secretary-Treasurer, United Givers Fund, Hancock County; Mrs. Gwen Guillot, Biloxi, Director, Tri-County Project on Aging; The Honorable Warren Carver, Mayor of Bay St. Louis, and Arthur Clementin, the Giles' grandson. Seated, l. to r., Eugene Giles, New Orleans, LA, Mrs. Giles' son; Mrs. Giles; and Rev. Charles Giles, the honoree's husband

The Award

Miss Irma introduced Mama Nettie to Mrs. C. W. Beyer, who was the Executive Secretary of the Hancock County United Fund. "Mrs. Giles has worked miracles with the children. She really has a special talent to reach them where no one else ever could. I think that she should receive some recognition for all the things she's done over the years to raise more than 40 children in her home," Miss Irma stated.

One day, Mama Nettie received a call from Mrs. Beyer. "Mrs. Giles, would you have time to stop by my office sometime tomorrow?"

"I'll have to bring some of my children with me, but I can stop by after school, if that's all right? Is this about next year's funding?" Mama Nettie asked.

"I'll explain everything to you when you get here, so we'll see you tomorrow."

That evening as she talked with Dad over the supper table, she told him about the call from Mrs. Beyer. "I wonder if the United Way Fund money is going to be cut next year?"

"Well, don't you go losing sleep over it," Dad replied. "You know that the Lord will provide if this thing is pleasing in His sight."

As usual, Mama Nettie prayed long after the lights were turned out for the night.

Morning rolled around quickly, and she was up, going through the normal routine before heading out for school. During the morning, she stopped by Miss Irma's desk for a moment.

"Do you know what's going on down at Mrs. Beyer's office?" she asked.

"Why no, I don't have a clue. You let me know what Mrs. Beyer has to say!"

That afternoon, Mama Nettie loaded the five Pearlington children into the car. Iris dropped off the Kiln and Delisle kids for her so she could attend the meeting with Mrs. Beyer. When she got to the office, she lined the children up in the reception area.

"Now you all sit quietly, and don't bother anything. I'll just be a few minutes."

Mama Nettie was escorted into Mrs. Beyer's office. To her amazement, Mrs. Beyer was not alone. There was a committee waiting to see her.

"Sit down, Mrs. Giles; I have something to tell you. You know Mayor Warren Carver and Miss Irma of course. Everyone sat around the room and greeted Mama Nettie. "Well," said Mrs. Beyer, "I know that you're wondering why I asked you to come today, so I will get right to the point. Mrs. Arnett Giles, I'm pleased to announce that we submitted your name for nomination, and you have been appointed the 1971 recipient of the National Volunteer of the Year Award."

Mama Nettie sat quietly, and in shock. "What does this mean?" she asked.

"It means, my dear, that you have been selected from people all over the United States as the greatest volunteer of the year. It means that you, your husband, and two of your family members will accompany you to Washington, D.C., where you will be honored at a special banquet. President Richard Nixon will present you with an award, and you will receive a check for $5,000 to spend any way you like. A committee from Bay St. Louis will be allowed to go along with you, too."

Mama Nettie was literally frozen, and words would not come to her lips. Silent tears streamed down her cheeks. The ladies each walked over to embrace her and the Mayor shook her hand.

"Mrs. Giles, there is not a more deserving person in the state of Mississippi or the entire nation. We are all proud, and honored, to know and work with you."

Mama Nettie regained her composure, and said, "I never would have expected this in a million years. You all know how I feel about the children. Everything that I have done has been for them. I vowed that I would never let any child be mistreated or unloved if there was something that I could do to help it. I never expected any laurels for doing what I could to serve the Lord, because He said in His word that we should do good for the least of our brothers."

There was a frenzy of excitement about town. News articles were spread throughout the counties, and congratulations were coming in from all across the country.

"Nettie, you'll need a fancy gown for the ball, so we're going to take you shopping," Mrs. Beyer said. Not only did they buy a beautiful pale yellow gown for the banquet, Mama Nettie came home with an entire wardrobe of beautiful dresses, suits, and matching jewelry.

Finally, the big day arrived. Dad and Uncle Gene accompanied Mama Nettie to Washington. This was Mama Nettie and Dad's first trip on an airplane. They were also accompanied by a delegation from Bay St. Louis, which included: Mrs. C. R. Beyer, Executive Secretary of the Hancock County United Fund; Mr. Warren Carver, Mayor of Bay St. Louis; Mr. Perry Gibson, President of the Hancock County Chamber of Commerce; Mrs. Frances Franckiewicz, Director of the Hancock County Welfare Department; Mrs. Gwen Ishim, friend of the family; and Mrs. Gwen Guillot, Chairman of the Council for the Aged of Hancock County.

Upon arrival in Washington, they were met at the airport and escorted to their hotel rooms. Art had graduated from Jackson State College in Jackson, Mississippi, and had taken a teaching position in Jackson, Michigan. He flew directly from Detroit to Washington, where he met up with the rest of the family early the following morning.

That day, they were taken to the office of Mississippi Senator Stennis, and given a private, guided tour of the White House, including the Oval Office. Later that evening, they were escorted to the John F. Kennedy Center for the Performing Arts for the banquet.

President Nixon presented my grandmother with a plaque. She was the first individual winner of the annual National Volunteer Award, and she was cited for her work with homeless, neglected and retarded children and for lending a helping hand to the elderly in her community. Nixon told several hundred volunteers at the gala black-tie event that people like Mrs. Giles represented something that's very special about this country. Her type of spirit is what distinguishes this country from others and makes it great.

Mrs. Eunice Kennedy Shriver, sister of the late President John F. Kennedy, presented Mama Nettie to the audience and gave her a check for $5,000.

Mama Nettie thanked the audience and said, "I am not used to giving speeches. I don't think that I'm able to find adequate words to express my gratitude. I can only give thanks to God. I want you all to know that everything I did was not to gain recognition. I have only been trying to follow in the steps of Christ. I don't really like all this publicity, but if I can inspire someone in my own way to help, then it is alright." She concluded by saying, "May God open your eyes, your hearts and your pocketbooks to help those in need."

Henry Ford, II remarked, "In so many ways, Arnette Giles has been a motivating force within her community – stimulating others to awareness and action, creating concern and understanding through her own unique and unselfish example. You know, it's amazing what one person like Mrs. Giles had done without even a feasibility study."

Though the room was filled with dignitaries and many important political officials, only two people received a standing ovation: President Nixon and Mrs. Arnette Giles. Throughout the event, Mama Nettie kept her warm smile. Dwight Cook, Master of Ceremonies, summed it up when he said, "Everybody Mrs. Giles has touched now knows how to smile."

The following day, Mama Nettie, Dad, Uncle Gene and Art were driven to New York City, where she and Art were interviewed on television. They taped three shows that day, and they were all given accommodations at the Waldorf Astoria for two nights.

"Well Mama, did you ever, in your wildest dreams, think that we would come all the way from Pearlington, Mississippi to dine with the President and shake hands with so many important people?" Dad asked, as they reposed in the posh bed at the Waldorf Astoria. "And now, here we are in New York City, too!"

"It is a bit overwhelming, but I'm glad that it happened if some good can come out of it. At least now, I have some money to do some of the things that I've dreamed about for the school. In fact, the first thing that I'm going to do when we get home is to buy a bigger car, so I can transport all of the children in one trip. I can buy supplies, and — "

"Now hold on Mama, it's $5,000, not $50,000. As far as I know, only the good Lord was able to feed the multitude with five loaves and two fish," Dad replied. They held hands in the dark and laughed out loud until the tears flowed, and the laughter soon turned to gentle slumber.

They spent the following day touring in New York, and the next morning, a limousine took them to the airport. Art gave Mama Nettie and Dad a big hug at the terminal.

"I'm so proud of you both!" he said. He turned to Uncle Gene and gave him a hug. "Well Unc, you take good care of the old folks." With that, he turned to find the gate for his trip back to Detroit.

After Art's graduation from Valena C. Jones High School in 1965, Dad sold one of the cows to pay for his first semester of tuition at Jackson State College. Art graduated with a degree in industrial technology in 1969, and he taught for one year at a junior high school in Hattiesburg, Mississippi.

The following year, Art moved to Jackson, Michigan where he taught drafting and technical drawing at Jackson Parkside High School. He took a job as a scout for the National Football League from 1980 to 1983. In 1983, he accepted the position of Assistant Principal of the Jackson Area Career Center, a vocational high school, in Jackson, Michigan.

Art earned a Master's Degree in 1988 and a Doctorate Degree in 1992 from Eastern Michigan University. He worked as an Administrator of the Jackson Area Career Center from 1983 to 2002. Art retired in 2002, and returned to the Mississippi Gulf Coast. He resides in Bay St. Louis. He is married to Laverne Haynes-Whavers and has five grown children: Michael, Michelle, Charles, Cynthia, and Arthur Phillip IV.

When Mama Nettie got back to Mississippi, she purchased a little red station wagon to transport her school kids, and she added more furniture and fixtures to the schoolroom to help the children's learning process. Things didn't quiet down for more than two years after the award.

Besides the hustle and bustle of her regular schedule, Mama Nettie was called upon to make guest appearances up and down the Gulf Coast. That Christmas, she was interviewed by *Life* Magazine, and they did a four-page article with pictures of the children. During the summer of 1972, two college students from Minnesota with aspirations to teach mentally handicapped children came to spend a week with Mama Nettie. They interviewed her, and they followed her around to take notes on her methods with the children.

In June 1974, Mama Nettie suffered a detached retina. She endured surgery and the torturous aftercare of having to lie flat on her back for two weeks, with her head wedged between bricks. The first surgery didn't work, so within a few months she had a second procedure. She had cataracts too, and after their removal her vision got somewhat better, but she never regained her good sight.

Chapter XIV

Dying Season

Shannon Marie

I was pregnant in 1973, and we were all anticipating the birth of my fifth child. All of my children had small birth weights. Julie, my second child was six weeks premature and weighed only three pounds, ten ounces. I went into premature labor, and Shannon Marie was born on April 23, 1973. They took her from the delivery room and rushed to get her connected to a respirator. We were told that her lungs were not developed enough to function without assistance.

I pleaded with the doctors to let me see my baby, but I wasn't allowed out of bed the first day. On the morning of the second day, I walked down the hall to the nursery. She was so tiny, and frail, and like Julie, she weighed just over three pounds. About ten o'clock that morning, the pediatrician came in to talk to me, and she said that Shannon appeared to be stabilizing, and she felt confident that she would be much better by the following morning.

I shared a room with another mother, and when they brought her baby in, I cried for my little girl. Around eleven o'clock that morning, the nurses came in and began moving my things.

"We're taking you to a private room," the nurse said.

"Why? I didn't request a private room. My insurance will not cover it." They remained mute. Suddenly, a cold fist gripped my heart and fear paralyzed my body. "What's wrong? Is something wrong with my baby?" Without a word, they moved me into the private room, and I was told that the doctor would come in to speak to me. I knew then that my baby was dead.

The pediatrician came in, and told me that my baby had suffered a cerebral hemorrhage. The doctor asked me if I would sign a waiver to let them perform an autopsy.

"It might give us some insight into why you deliver early, and it could possibly be of help should you have any future pregnancies."

"Will they give me my baby after the autopsy? I want to bury her."

"I'm afraid that's not possible."

"Then what will they do with her?" I asked.

"Well, the hospital will dispose of the body."

I don't remember much around me after that. I started screaming, "No, you can't have my baby, you're not going to chop her into pieces and throw her in the incinerator," I shouted. With that, they came in and sedated me, and I stayed that way for a couple of days.

My husband took me to Mama Nettie's house, and she held me through the night as I cried for the sweet little girl that I had carried and loved. Depression spread over me, and I was plagued with nightmares.

Two days after I was discharged from the hospital, Shannon Marie was released to the funeral home. They brought her tiny, little white coffin to the house, and set her on the coffee table. I sat in a chair next to her, and caressed her tiny, cold fingers.

God! Why did you take her from me? I thought. I sat there for about two hours. Mama Nettie brought the other children in to see their baby sister.

Finally, the undertaker said, "I'm sorry, but we must take her to the cemetery now."

Uncle Gene had come out to Pearlington the day before, and constructed a tiny tomb, which sat on top of Papa Phillip's grave. I was still too weak and too sedated to leave the house, so I stayed home while the parish priest accompanied my family to the cemetery.

I returned to work after two months, but the pain never subsided. I was plagued with the same nightmare every night. In my dream, Papa Phillip was marching from the cemetery to the house. He was dressed in the same black suit that he wore in the picture that hung on Mama Nettie's bedroom wall, and in his arms he held my baby, Shannon Marie. I would awake from my dream in a cold sweat.

Dad Goes Home

Six months later, in October 1974, tragedy struck again. Dad woke one Sunday morning, and after our usual Sunday breakfast and prayer service, he got dressed for church. I was standing at the kitchen sink, washing up the breakfast dishes. I turned to see him sitting on the foot of one of the twin beds in the kids' room, which was just off the kitchen.

"Are you all right, old man?" I asked.

"I guess so," he replied. "I never knew what you and Mama suffered all these years with your headaches, but today, for the first time in my life, I have one."

I was really worried. He looked so frail and fragile, sitting there on the foot of that bed. I wanted to go over and put my arms around his neck and tell him how much I loved him. I was afraid to allow myself to think that Dad might be close to death. He had been the only father that I had ever really known. I had watched him slaughter 300-pound hogs, and tug the 500-pound cows through the marsh. I had watched him split giant logs for the wood stove and carry 50-pound sacks of feed on his shoulders. He had always been an invincible giant to me, and now the thought that his mortality might be dwindling was too much to bear.

I was living in New Orleans then, and I spent my weekends in Pearlington with them. I returned home that night. Mama Nettie called Dad's doctor early Monday morning, and my Aunt Myrtle drove him to his appointment on Tuesday morning.

Dr. Diamond admitted him to Slidell Memorial Hospital for a series of tests. They discovered that the headache was indeed the result of a small stroke. The battery of tests left him exhausted, but he was in good spirits and never lost his ever-pleasant good humor.

I called to chat with him, and told him that I was on my way to pay him a visit.

"Now don't you go getting on that highway this time of night. I'll see you Friday night when you come home. Your brother just called, too, and I've got a room full of company," Dad told me. Mama Nettie, Mama, Aunt Myrtle and Uncle Gene were all in the room with him.

Not more than an hour after speaking to Dad, Mama called me back to tell me that he was dead. "He was talking to us and laughing. All of a sudden, a bright halo seemed to appear around his face. He leaned forward for a second and when he fell back to the pillow, he was gone," Mama said.

I don't know how I drove down the highway that night. The tears flowed down my cheeks, and I filled the car with my screams. "Scamp, Scamp," I cried. How could you leave us?" I wept for my dear grandmother who had just lost her companion of 54 years. Despite Dad's defects and handicaps, he was the love of her life. My grandmother's words rang in my ears, "A half loaf that loves you is better than a whole loaf that doesn't." I wondered, too, if I would ever find that kind of love.

I pulled in the side lane between the old house and the Odd Fellows Hall, and I sat there in the dark for a while until I could stop my own agony. Mama Nettie had always been there for me and for everyone else. I wanted to be strong for her now, so I took a deep breath and headed for the back door.

Everyone was sitting in the dining room. My grand-mother sat staring down at her wedding band, as she twisted it around on her finger. The house was filled with a strange light. Even the house felt different, as if the very walls were missing their master. The house was filled with sorrow. Yet, no one cried, no one spoke.

I went over to my grandmother and knelt at her feet. I laid my head on her lap and put my arms around her lower back. I finally raised my head to look into her eyes, and I said, "I'm so sorry!"

She looked down at me and caressed my hair. "I know," she whispered. "I know." We stayed that way for a long while, and as I knelt there, I prayed that God would drain the pain from her, and pass it on to me.

The next few days were hazy. There were hundreds of phone calls to make, and hundreds to receive. I stayed close to the house while Mama and her sister and brothers took Mama Nettie to the funeral home, and wherever else she needed to go to finalize the funeral arrangements.

I learned later that the hospital had performed an autopsy on my grandfather, and they left his scalp peeled down over his eyes. Just before releasing his body to the funeral home, they allowed my grandmother to go in to see him. Luckily, Mama and Aunt Myrtle were with her, because when my grandmother got a look at her husband her knees buckled under her. That was really an inhumane act on the part of the hospital, and my mother gave them wrath for a long time.

Finally, the eve of the funeral arrived. It is the custom in our area of the south to conduct a Wake Service the night before the funeral. The Protestant wake services are always a long, drawn out affair. There are hymns, and speeches, and lots of moaning and weeping. I had attended my share of funerals with my grandparents when I was a little girl. Later, after I started attending Catholic School, we sang the Requiem Mass at every funeral in the parish. I made a promise to myself that I wouldn't go to another funeral once I became an adult. Until now, I had kept that promise, but this was Dad.

Everyone got dressed in black, and it was nearly time to leave for the church. I hesitated for a moment, and then I knocked on Mama Nettie's bedroom door.

"May I come in for a minute?" I asked. She was sitting on her bed, and I sat next to her and placed my hands over hers. "Mama Nettie, you know how I feel about funerals. I really don't want to go, but if you want me to be there, I'll go for you."

She lifted her right hand and placed it to my cheek. "You don't have to go. Someone should be at the house anyway, in case someone comes by or phones for directions to the church."

I removed her hand from my cheek and kissed it. Then, I put my arms around her neck and hugged her for a few minutes. All these years, I had felt safe and comforted in the gentle shelter of her arms, and now it was my turn to give her comfort.

It was after midnight when everyone returned from the church. Mama Nettie was exhausted, but she sat in the kitchen for several hours.

"Go to bed!" she told me. In my usual manner, I had tried to keep her company, but I guess she just wanted time to be alone with her memories.

There were still three foster children in the house: Tommy, Tony, and Gary, and the two adopted children: Gina, and Kenny. In addition, I had my four children: Craig, Julie, Shaun, and Jeremy. I got up early to get everyone fed, showered and dressed for the funeral. I remained at the house to make beds, and receive the tons of food that friends and neighbors dropped off. When the phone and the door were silent, I said a prayer for my grandmother.

Chapter XV

Learning to Crawl

A Period of Discovery

After Dad's death, the life seemed to drain out of my grandmother. Dad had looked out for the kids while she worked, so she made the decision to stop teaching in order to stay at home with her children. Meanwhile, her eyesight continued to deteriorate.

I decided to move back to Pearlington that year. I wanted to be close to my grandmother, and I wanted to help her in any way I could. I brought her medicine and gave her pedicures, which had always been my job as long as I can remember. She had been sick for 11 years with the blood disease, but as her failing eyesight continued to progress, she could no longer drive. Gina was 16 and had a license, so she did all of the driving now. Mama Nettie never uttered a word of complaint, but I could see the sadness in her eyes.

With further loss of her eyesight, Mama Nettie had to give up the three foster children. Gary, the youngest of the three, was autistic, and he required an exhausting amount of attention. When he came to them a few years earlier he didn't speak, but he made high-pitched screams and screeches. He was suffering from malnutrition, and he had been physically abused. Gary was seven, but he was smaller than my two-year-old. He had been locked in a dark room and kept chained to a bed. Initially, the doctors thought that he was deaf, but as Mama Nettie worked with him, she began to notice that he reacted to sounds.

On Christmas of 1973, Gary pronounced his first word, "Ball!"

You would have thought that he had just recited the Declaration of Independence. Loud shouts of joy and claps rang throughout the house, and tears welled up in Mama Nettie's eyes. She had broken another wild horse. We didn't know it then, but Gary was the last child to benefit from my grandmother's special talents.

Dad had been laid to rest about three weeks when I accompanied my grandmother to the cemetery, one brisk fall day. We pulled weeds and grass from the gravesites of everyone in the family plot, and Mama Nettie put two large plants of waxed, pink begonias at the base of Dad's tomb. We were preparing the graves for the November 1st feast of All Saints Day. It is the custom in our area to whitewash the tombs and place flowers on the graves. On November 2nd, All Souls Day, the priest goes to the cemetery to bless the graves, and we always pray for our deceased loved ones. Everything was clean and ready for the ceremony.

I was standing at the kitchen sink washing breakfast dishes when the telephone rang. I could hear my grandmother in the background, but I could not quite understand the gist of her conversation. I knew that she was talking to someone at the cemetery, and for some reason, a cold chill ran through me.

When she hung up, she said to me, "Come over here and sit down for a minute. I have something to tell you, but I don't want you to get upset." My mind sped, and I wondered what could upset me at the cemetery. "That was the cemetery caretaker," she said. "Last night, someone vandalized a number of graves, and one of them was Shannon's.

I sat frozen in disbelief. I couldn't speak. Tears filled my eyes, and my throat felt as if a golf ball had been wedged in my esophagus. I was having difficulty breathing. I jumped up from the kitchen table and ran towards the back door. Dad's old single-barrel shotgun still stood behind the door.

I grabbed the gun and attempted to cross the threshold, but Mama Nettie reached out and grabbed me by the back of my shirt.

"Hold it!" she yelled. "Where are you going?"

"I'm going to the cemetery," I replied, and I attempted to pull away from her.

"Hold on!" she yelled as she tightened her grip on me. "Who are you going to kill? Everybody's already dead down there."

Somehow her words snapped me into reality, and I handed over the gun. My grandmother took me into her bedroom, and let me cry until I had enough courage to go down to the cemetery. The vandals had removed Shannon's tiny little coffin from her final resting place, opened it, and left it sitting in the middle of the lane about 200 feet from her tomb. When we reached the cemetery, the Sheriff was already there. They closed the coffin and returned it to the tomb, and the caretaker went off to get cement to reseal it.

The grave desecration had transpired on Halloween night. My nightmares continued, but the new ones included some satanic group performing evil rituals on my sweet baby's body. If I was headed toward healing before, this incident set me back and sent me into a deeper depression. I clung to my pain for 22 years before I finally let go, and laid my little girl to rest. I grew to dread and hate

Halloween, and even now that I've surpassed the pain, I still can't help but think about that event whenever October 31st rolls around.

I stayed close to my grandmother for the next two years. We spent hours laughing, and talking. During that period, I came to realize that age was a definite state of mind. Prior to this period, I always thought that the mind aged in tune with the body, but I discovered that the mind remains young and vibrant even though it becomes entrapped in an aging and ailing body. Now, as I write and realize that I am swiftly approaching old age, I can certainly reaffirm my revised theory on the aging mind.

I loved hearing the old stories about our ancestors, and the ancient ways handed down from past generations. I asked about our Choctaw heritage, and I wanted to know what had happened to everyone. I wanted to hear about the happy occasions and the hard times, too. I wanted to know why my grandmother had become the person she was, and what motivated her to keep going. I wanted to stamp every story deep into my memory so that I could pass them down to my children. I had heard many things dozens of times, but they always seemed fresh and exciting to me.

Letting Go

On Memorial Day of 1976, I slept in a little later than usual. Every day I was up at five o'clock in the morning to get the kids up, and get on the highway by six-thirty for my hour-long commute to New Orleans. I got up at eight because the kids were already getting restless. They wanted to go to the beach for a picnic. By ten o'clock, we had packed a lunch, and everyone was ready to head out to Gulfside. I walked over to Mama Nettie's house to ask if she wanted to go with us.

To my surprise, the front door was locked. I walked around to the side door, and it was locked too. The house was quiet. Where could they be? I noticed that the car was gone from the lane. I went back to the house, and we left for the beach. All day, I had a strange feeling in the pit of my stomach, and I called my mother to see if she knew where they were.

We got home from the beach around six-thirty that evening, and the telephone was ringing when I put the key in the door. It was Gina.

"Can you come quickly? Mama got sick, and I took her to the emergency room in Slidell."

I had a million questions for her. Where was she all day? When did you take her to the hospital, and what's wrong with her? Both Mama and Aunt Myrtle worked at Slidell Hospital. I called Mama at work, and told her that Mama Nettie was down in the emergency room. By the time I got to the hospital, they had already admitted my grandmother to a room.

Test results indicated that she was suffering from septic shock, and her vital organs were shutting down quickly. I went home that night and made arrangements for my children. The next morning, I returned to the hospital, and remained there for three days until Mama Nettie took her last breath on June 4, 1976. The doctors said that she was in a coma, but she did come around for a while on the second day. She knew where she was, and called her doctor by name. During that period, I sat holding her hand and telling her how much I loved her.

Mama Nettie always told me that she would never leave me as long as I needed her. I had always been dependent on her for the love and moral support that only she could give unconditionally. At first I cried, and begged her not to leave me. I reminded her of her promise to me, and I told her that I was not ready. I was only 28 years old.

On the morning of the third day, her breathing became shallow, and when I lifted the sheet to untangle her foot, I noticed large blisters on her heels. Her whole body was becoming infiltrated with the fluids that they were pumping into her.

Although she had oxygen, she tugged constantly at the tube. At that point, I realized how selfish I was. My poor grandmother had sacrificed her entire life for others, and she had probably given me the greatest sum of her tireless energy and love. I held her hand, and leaned close to whisper in her ear.

"If you're ready, and you really want to go, I will be all right. You don't have to stay for me. Thank you for everything that you've given me, and I will love you, and remember you forever."

I continued to sit next to the bed as she began to take those long labored breaths. I held my breath too, during those endless spans of inhaling and exhaling. When she took her last breath, I waited for the sound of life to resume, but she was gone. I sat there for a while, and I bent over her to give her one last kiss, one last hug.

I walked out to the parking lot and sat in my car for a moment. The light was brilliant, and as I looked up at the billowing clouds, I'm positive that I saw Mama Nettie and Dad, walking hand-in-hand. I thought that I could hear Dad say, "Well, Mama, now I can get some hot biscuits tomorrow morning." I smiled as I started the car, and headed home to tell my children that their great-grand-mother had gone to heaven.

There was never any doubt in my mind that everyone loved Mama Nettie as much as I did. There was such a diverse crowd of people who sent condolences to the family. Politicians, co-workers, and friends came from far and near to pay final homage to her, but the people she surely smiled down upon must have been all of her children, who turned out in hoards to get one last glimpse of Mama Nettie. I was so happy that she had received that recognition while she was alive. She always said in her humility, "I never expected laurels for the things that I did out of love."

True to myself, I didn't attend Mama Nettie's funeral either. I will always remember her smile, her laughter, and the gentleness of her touch. She's been gone over 30 years, and I can still feel her near me. I can still hear her wise words of encouragement.

"No mountain's too high to climb. No sea is too deep to swim. Put yourself in the Lord's hands, and He will give you your heart's desire.

Mama Nettie and Dad are resting together now in their side-by-side tombs in Pearlington Cemetery.

Time to Grow Up

I was completely devastated after the death of my grandmother. I was fearful that some tragedy would befall me, and I would have no one to console or encourage me. I was also ashamed that a 28-year-old mother of four was afraid to stand up on her own two feet. Something had to change, and I knew that the change would have to be me. I could no longer have the mind of a child. It was time for me to grow up.

I took a deep breath and said to myself out loud, "You can do this. You have everything that you need. You're young, beautiful, intelligent, and one of Mama Nettie's children." I opened the door of opportunity and stepped out into the world.

I counted one, two three. I had lost Dad, Shannon, and now my grandmother. If I had to rate the measure of sorrow, I guess the loss of my child had toughened me up for what was yet to come. My husband, Maurice, would pass a few short years later in a tragic automobile accident. I did everything under the sun to block the memory of his death from my heart and my mind. However, it literally took five years, relocating five thousand miles away, and the happy conclusion of a reoccurring dream to finally put my heart at ease.

Epilogue

"Hey, Sis, Sis," I heard Art's voice calling from the van. "Did you plan on spending the night here? I know that you had a lot of catching up to do, but it's getting late."

I gave the tomb one last pat and turned to join my brother. "Oh, I'm so sorry. I guess I got lost in my memories. We can go now. Those old folks aren't here anyway."

"Don't worry," Art replied. "I must have dozed off for a minute myself. I'm about ready for some dinner, how about you?"

"That sounds like a plan," I said.

Art fired up the engine, and we paused for a second to stare at yet another of Hurricane Katrina's works. A big yellow house still sat in the middle of the road about a hundred feet from the entrance to the cemetery. "I wonder where that house came from, because I just don't remember it being anyplace around here."

I sat in silence for a while longer, and the past continued to flash through my mind. I knew every inch of this land. I had walked every road hundreds of times. Even though there was so much obvious destruction, the eternally imprinted pictures in my mind still played tricks on me and I could somehow envision things as they had once been when my life was so simple and so peaceful.

I thought about all of the people, living and passed, who my dear grandparents had helped or influenced in some special way. It made me realize how rich they had become through their good works. "I don't need any rewards now," Mama Nettie always said, "I'll wait for the stars on my crown when I get to heaven."

I know she's wearing that brilliant crown now, but surely all of us who benefited physically, morally and spiritually from her presence are the true shining jewels of her crown. Arnette Thelma Peters-Giles lived an exemplary life. She had literally walked in the spirit of Jesus.

I reached over to touch my brother's large hand, and I smiled to myself as I realized how foolish I'd been to worry about the dead. It's not about the land or the things that we've accumulated. It's not even about the dust that we leave when we're gone. It's the love that endures though time and space, through destruction and even death. That's what Mama Nettie tried to teach us, and I had finally gotten it.

As we drove down the road, I looked up at my brother and said, "Well, I guess since we're the old folks now, it's up to us to carry on Mama Nettie's legacy to our children."

The End

Resources

❀❀❀

Kidwell, Clara Sue (c1995). <u>Choctaws and Missionaries in Mississippi, 1818-1918.</u> University of Oklahoma Press

Maxson, Etienne William (1955). <u>The Progress of the Races</u>. McQuiddy Printing Company, Nashville, TN

Schariff, Robert G. (1999). <u>Louisiana's Loss, Mississippi's Gain (A History of Hancock County Mississippi from the Stone Age to the Space Age)</u>. Brunswick Publishing Company, Lawrenceville, VA

Smith, John David (1996). <u>Black Voices from Reconstruction 1865-1877</u>. The Mill Press, Brookfield, Connecticut

Thigpen, S. G. (c1965). <u>Pearl River: Highway to Glory Land</u>. Kingsport Press, Kingsport, TN.

A Publication of the Mississippi Department of Public Welfare (1972).<u>The Welfare Brief.</u> Volume IV, No. 12

Research Sources

Encyclopedia.com

Hancock County Historical Society, Bay St. Louis, MS

Hancock County Marriage Records, Court House - Bay St. Louis, MS

Hancock County Property Deeds and Records Office, Court House - Bay St. Louis, MS

Hancock County Public Library, Bay St. Louis, MS

Louisiana State University Library

The Sea Coast Echo Archives (stored at the public library), Bay St. Louis, MS

United States Federal Census Records